The Collectible John Steinbeck

The Collectible John Steinbeck

A Practical Guide

Compiled by
Robert B. Harmon

McFarland & Company, Inc., Publishers
Jefferson, North Carolina, and London

Library of Congress Cataloguing-in-Publication Data

Harmon, Robert B. (Robert Bartlett), 1932–
The collectible John Steinbeck.

Bibliography: p.185
Includes index.
1. Steinbeck, John, 1902–1968 – Bibliography.
2. Book Collecting. 3. Book – Prices. I. Steinbeck, John, 1902–1968. II. Title.
Z8839.4.H28 1986 [PS3537.T3234] 016.813'52 85-43578

ISBN 0-89950-206-7 (acid-free natural paper)

Manufactured in the United States of America.

McFarland Box 611 Jefferson NC 28640

Dedicated affectionately to Merlynn

Acknowledgments

The material for this book was drawn from a wide variety of sources. The illustrations from books published by The Viking Press are reprinted here by arrangement with Viking Penguin Inc. The entire group was photographed from the superb collection in the Steinbeck Research Center at San Jose State University, San Jose, California, with the permission of Dr. Robert DeMott, Director; Maureen Pastine, University Librarian; and Bernadine Beutler, Head, Special Collections Department. A special expression of gratitude is due to my good friend Donald E. Fletcher for his skill and patience in photographing these materials.

Bibliographic and descriptive material not immediately available to me was gathered from the sources indicated in the body of the text.

Table of Contents

Introduction

It is a good idea at the outset to understand just what is meant by the term "book collecting." While there is no clear consensus among practitioners, the term may be defined as follows: the formation of a special kind of collection or library which reflects the personal interests of the collector, and where books are regarded both as objects in themselves and texts to be read. The collecting impulse, then, is usually initiated by a love of words within the books. The avid collector displays many qualities in the building of a fine collection. He or she learns all that is possible about his or her field of interest, and then exercises taste and judgment when acquiring desired materials. Collectors also strive to make their collections as comprehensive and high in quality as possible.

Being hooked on collecting materials by and about famous American writers is a strange malady that infects one long before he or she is ever consciously aware of it. As a natural consequence, by the time the problem is discovered and identified it is impossible to do anything about it. This is especially true of those interested in John Steinbeck. Once one has been bitten by the Steinbeck bug, the desire to collect everything by and about him becomes insatiable and incurable. While Steinbeck collecting is in essence no different than that for other great American writers, there seems to exist a special intensity and sense of purpose among Steinbeck enthusiasts. This phenomenon is not easy to define in concrete terms, but it is none the less quite evident to those so engaged.

Beginning in the early 1960s, just a few years before Steinbeck's death, a renewed interest in his work became evident on several levels. An upsurge in scholarly interest was followed by an increased demand by the common reader for his works. As a result, the demand for collectible Steinbeck editions also intensified. Currently we are witnessing an acceleration of this demand, along with high prices and an ever-diminishing supply of certain Steinbeck editions.

Some problems always seem to plague collectors. One of the more perplexing difficulties is the identification of collectible editions; another is determination of a fair price for such items. For a number of years, Steinbeck collectors had very little help in either area. In 1974, however, the Goldstone-Payne bibliography was published and provided much-needed descriptive and other bibliographic information. Five years later, this bibliographer published a brief pocket guide to Steinbeck's first editions. Notwithstanding their usefulness, both of these works have their limitations. The former is not complete and contains a number of errors; the latter contains some errors and covers only first editions.

The book you are holding attempts to correct these errors and to provide you with adequate descriptive information on as many Steinbeck collectible editions as are contained in available sources. To accomplish this, an extensive and careful search has been conducted to discover and identify the various English-language Steinbeck editions of a collectible nature. Within certain physical and bibliographical limitations, accuracy has been stressed. Added to this is an attempt to provide you (where possible) with some idea of the range of prices currently being asked by booksellers and others for specific Steinbeck editions. Also discussed are the dynamics of Steinbeck collecting, accompanied by some helpful hints on how to go about searching for materials.

I. The Collection Process

1. The Dynamics of Steinbeck Collecting

More than ever before, book collecting is a grand love affair, in which, to paraphrase John Steinbeck, everybody gets kissed.[1] To those so engaged, book collecting is a most exhilarating and pleasurable experience. Once hooked, few ever outgrow it because its possibilities are infinite, and more often than not, the enjoyment derived from collecting books increases rather than diminishes with the passing of time. One finds that the desire to collect has a sort of mystical quality about it, indeed a kind of religious aura that eventually becomes an integral part of one's life and at times overrules one's common sense and more practical modes of action.[2]

One may wonder why we want to collect the works by and about a specific author such as John Steinbeck. What makes these materials so desirable? Some believe it inevitable that sooner or later those collectors whose tastes follow current fashion will stampede after Steinbeck.[3] Yet others over the years have viewed the Steinbeck phenomenon as only a passing infatuation that will sputter and die out in time. Predictors of diminshed interest seem to have misjudged the holding power of the Steinbeck mystique, for he appears to be as popular as ever today, not only with the American reading public but abroad as well.

To understand why Steinbeckiana enjoys such a high level of collectibility it will be helpful first to look at the main reasons why Steinbeck has such wide appeal for readers. Quite simply, Steinbeck has the basic ingredients of good literature. Ultimately, all good literature is just a combination of two things: words and truth, and great writers have been able to combine them successfully.[4]

It should be obvious to anyone who has come in contact with Steinbeck's writing that it is transparently easy to read. Few people have to reread his sentences or repeat his paragraphs. Most readers find that they remember his stories, if not all the smallest details, many years after a single reading. However, being easy to read is not enough. Dullness may be easy to read. An author must have something to say. If it touches the universal soul of humankind, the author can even get by with turgid style or obscure composition. But if a person writes with an art that conceals the art and in so doing strikes a common chord in our humanity, then the author can appeal to anyone who can read at all. If you cannot read Steinbeck, you cannot read.[5]

From his youth John Steinbeck liked to hear and tell stories, and his skill in relating good ones spilled over into his writing. Almost inevitably his stories and novels deal with such basic human themes and conflicts as the struggle of good *vs.* evil, free will *vs.* fate, and the Judeo-Christian ethic *vs.* the Darwinian universe. Steinbeck's humorous and sympathetic view of human nature tends to confirm rather than condemn humanity, which creates a friendly bond with his readers.[6]

Steinbeck had a knack of creating original and fascinating characters who are both believable and unforgettable. The vitality of these character types shows his love of people. He also had a profound love of the land and a deep interest in the organic relationships between all forms and conditions of life. Indeed it has been said that Steinbeck's ecological insights with respect to the relationship between humankind and nature were nearly forty years ahead of his time.[7]

It was not uncommon for John Steinbeck to express his love for America and to strongly support freedom of expression. He thus became a representative American commentator and popular philosopher, and as a cultural ambassador to Russia he articulately defended democratic principles under presidents Kennedy and Johnson.[8]

To summarize, the collectibility of Steinbeck materials can be directly attributed to the fine quality of his writing. He was a masterful artist in combining words and truth. His understanding of the nature of the human condition, and his ability to tell a superb story, to create memorable characters, and to put it all in readable prose have made his literature appealing to a broad international audience. Add to this the enduring relevance of his message and perhaps we can appreciate more clearly his contribution to American literature.

John Steinbeck also rates well among the collectible authors of this century because of the wide range of his writings, the many reprintings of his books, and the wealth of writings about him and his career.[9] The determination of what to collect out of all this material is important. The following classification scheme suggests a framework for Steinbeck collectible materials. From it you can perhaps map out a collection strategy that suits your purpose. Keep in mind that these categories are not mutually exclusive, and some of the examples provided can fit into more than one group.[10]

Holograph Material

Holograph items include any material which is entirely in the author's handwriting—correspondence, diaries, account books, ledgers, manuscripts, and the like.

Limited Editions

These cover a stated number of copies printed of an item. Generally the copies are numbered consecutively and mostly signed by the author. Some examples include: *In Dubious Battle* (1936), 99 numbered and signed copies; *The Red Pony* (1937), 699 numbered and signed copies; *East of Eden* (1952), 1500 numbered and signed copies; *Un Américain à New-York et à Paris* (1956), 30 numbered and signed copies; *The Winter of Our Discontent* (1961), 500 copies; *Journal of a Novel* (1969), 600 copies; and *Steinbeck: A Life in Letters* (1975), 1000 copies.

Advance (proof) Copies

These are copies of a book, usually in wrappers, that are sent out to newspaper and magazine reviewers in advance of publication. Some known examples are: *Tortilla Flat* (1935); *Sea of Cortez* (1941); *The Moon Is Down* (1942); *Cannery Row* (1945); and *Sweet Thursday* (1954).

Salesman's Dummy Copies

A salesman's dummy is a facsimile copy of a published book, usually in a trade binding with the front matter and only a few pages of printed text. The remainder of the pages are blank. These copies were used for advertising purposes by book salesmen. Some known examples include: *Tortilla Flat. A Play* (1937); *Of Mice and Men* (1937); *Of Mice and Men. Play* (1937); *The Grapes of Wrath* (1939); *Sea of Cortez* (1941); and *The Moon Is Down* (1942).

Special or Private Printings

These are usually short publications issued by private presses, organizations, or by trade publishers for special occasions. Normally such special publications are numbered and signed by the author, but not always. Some good examples are: *Nothing So Monstrous* (1936), 370 copies signed by the author; *Saint Katy the Virgin* (1936), 199 numbered and signed copies; *John Steinbeck Replies* (1940); *How Edith McGillcuddy Met RLS* (1943), 152 copies; *Vanderbilt Clinic* (1947); *The First Watch* (1947), 60 numbered copies signed by the author; and *John Steinbeck His Language* (1970), 150 copies printed.

Special Limited Editions

These differ from the normal limited editions in that they are published by specialized organizations, such as the Limited Editions Club, the Franklin Library, etc. Several good examples are: *The Grapes of Wrath* (1940), Limited Editions Club, 2 volumes, 1146 copies printed; *Of Mice and Men* (1970), 1500 copies printed by the Limited Editions Club; *Sea of Cortez* (1971), published by Paul R. Appel in an edition of 750 copies; *Tortilla Flat* (1971), published by the Franklin Library.

First Regular Trade Editions

These include the first printings of a book distributed to bookstores for sale. However, a first edition may have several *issues*, the first normally being the most valuable. Issues are created when some kind of alteration of the type occurs during the printing of the first edition. Furthermore, an issue itself may have a separate *state* caused by a change in the book's binding, damaged type, inclusion of an errata slip, etc. Examples include *The Moon Is Down* (1942), which has two states of the dust jacket binding, as well as some differences in the type; and *The Pastures of Heaven* (1932), which has three different issues using the same printed sheets with a few exceptions. Copies signed or otherwise inscribed by the author are the most collectible. Unsigned first printings still have a great collectibility, with the author's first book being the most valuable. (Steinbeck is no exception; *Cup of Gold* [1929] is very much in demand and is extremely scarce, especially in good condition and with a dust jacket.)

Reprint Editions

Over the years since John Steinbeck published his first novel, many of his titles have been reproduced in reprint editions by various publishers. Some of the most prominent are P.F. Collier, The Sun Dial Press, Blue Ribbon Books (Canadian), Triangle, Heron Books (British), Grosset & Dunlap, Modern Library, Reprint Society (British), World Publishing Co. (Tower Books), Heritage Press, Garden City Publishing Co., Quality Press (British), and Armed Services Editions. Of marginal collectible value are reprints of reprints such as those offered by Folcroft Library Editions, Norwood Editions, and Richard West.

Book and Readers Club Editions

These editions could be considered reprints, but they are of significant quality to merit a separate category. Steinbeck works have been featured prominently in the following book club editions: Book-of-the-Month Club, Doubleday Dollar Book Club, Sears Readers Club, International Collector's Library, Book League of America, and the Literary Guild of America.

Condensed and Abridged Books

There are several series that included condensed or abridged versions of Steinbeck titles. They are particularly collectible if found in good condition and with original dust jackets. Some examples include Reader's Digest Association Condensed Books, *East of Eden* (1952), and *The Winter of Our Discontent* (1961); Books Abridged (British), *Once There Was a War* (1959), *The Short Reign of Pippin IV* (1957), and *Sweet Thursday* (1955).

Collected Works

Several series of collected Steinbeck works have appeared which contain selected short stories, excerpts from some novels, published correspondence, and the like. The value of these collections is greatly affected by the presence of dust jackets and the overall condition of the book. Some representative examples are *The Viking Portable Library Steinbeck* (1943, 1946, and 1971 editions); *The Steinbeck Omnibus* (1950, British); *The Indispensible Steinbeck* (1951); and *The Steinbeck Pocket Book* (1943).

Foreign English Language Editions

Many Steinbeck titles have been published in Great Britain and Canada. British editions mostly have been published by William Heinemann, Ltd. In Canada the major publisher has been Macmillan Co., Ltd., in Toronto although early titles were published by McLeod. These Canadian editions seem to be particularly collectible because they are very difficult to find. Two other European series are also very valuable. They are Continental Book Company's Zephyr Books editions such as *The Grapes of Wrath*, No. 28 in the series, and the Albatross editions such as *The Long Valley*, No. 509 in the series.

Foreign Language Editions

These editions present a particular challenge to the Steinbeck collector. Many of Steinbeck's works have been published in over thirty languages. In most cases they are specially illustrated and/or attractively bound. Also, several specific titles were first published in foreign languages and only translated into English later, such as *Positano* (1955). *Un Américain à New-York et à Paris* (1956) was published only in the French language.

Forewords, Introductions, Prefaces, Etc.

Steinbeck was frequently requested to contribute a foreword, introduction, or preface for the works of other authors. Only occasionally would he consent to do so. Some good examples are *Foreword to* "Between Pacific Tides" (1948); an introduction to Al Capp's *The World of Li'l Abner* (1953); and a preface to *Story Writing* (1962), by one of his former teachers at Stanford, Edith Ronald Mirrielees.

Endorsements

Somewhat related to his contributions to the works of other writers are Steinbeck's even more infrequent published endorsements of products or of books by other writers. Several examples include: an endorsement for Ballantine ale, *Life* 34, no. 4 (January 26, 1953): 92–93; an endorsement on the dust jacket of Dennis Murphy's book *The Sergeant* (1958); and an endorsement on the dust jacket of John Hargrave's book *Summer Time Ends* (1935). These collectible endorsements are very hard to find.

Anthologies

Steinbeck's short stories and excerpts from longer works have appeared in numerous anthologies. Because many of these have gone out of print, they have become collectors' items. Some representative examples include: *The Best Stories of 1938 and the Yearbook of the American Short Story* (1938), contains "The Chrysanthemums" on pages 277–287; and *The Best Plays of 1941–42 and the Yearbook of the Drama in America* (1942), contains *The Moon Is Down: a Play* (1942), on pages 72–108.

Pirated Editions

A pirated edition is any book published without the consent of the author. Such editions are produced and sold without the author's receiving any royalties. Since pirated editions are illegal to import, they are rare and provide a special inducement for the collector. An interesting example is a Taiwanese pirated edition of *The Winter of Our Discontent* (1961).

Published Correspondence

Just as Steinbeck's holographic letters are highly collectible, so also does his published correspondence enjoy a measure of value. Some good examples include: *John Steinbeck Replies* (1940); *A Letter from John Steinbeck* (1964); *Journal of a Novel* (1969); *John Steinbeck: His Language* (1970); and *Letters to Elizabeth* (1978).

Magazine or Periodical Contributions

A number of Steinbeck's short stories first appeared in periodicals and are collectible. A good example is Steinbeck's first article published for money, entitled "The Gifts of Iban" (by John Stern, pseud.), published in *The Smoker's Companion* 1, no. 1 (March 1927): 18–19, 70–72. Also from time to time Steinbeck wrote editorials such as "Atque Vale," which appeared in the *Saturday Review* 43, no. 30 (July 23, 1960): 13. Many of these are very difficult to find in good condition.

Paperback Editions

Over the past few years even paperback editions of Steinbeck's works have become highly desirable collectors' items. A prime example is the Armed Services Editions which were published for consumption by the American military during World War II. These are very much in demand and rarely are they advertised in booksellers' catalogs. Also of interest to the collector are the first, and in some cases, special paperback printings by Bantam, Dell, Modern Age, Penguin, etc. Perhaps the most important factor influencing the value of paperback editions, however, is *condition*.

Miscellaneous

There are some types of Steinbeck materials that do not fit neatly into identifiable groupings. Because of their value, however, it is necessary to mention them here. Take for example the scripts from various Steinbeck motion pictures such as "Lifeboat" (1944) and "A Medal for Benny" (1945). They are very scarce and quite valuable. There are large-print editions of certain works as well as a number published in braille for the blind. Steinbeck's speech accepting the Nobel Prize for Literature (1962), printed by Viking in pamphlet form, is a very collectible item if in good condition. In the past several years a fairly large mass of media materials has become available, some of it of collectible value. A good example is the recording of "The Snake" and "Johnny Bear" recorded by Steinbeck for Columbia Records and released in 1955. There are also cassette tapes of lectures by prominent Steinbeck scholars, filmstrips, and various combinations of instructional materials about Steinbeck country. Then there is the rather large category of Steinbeck ephemera, which includes such materials as photographs, drawings, paintings, playbills, ads, newspaper articles, and other personal belongings of the author. These can include such things as drivers' licenses, marriage certificates, birth certificates, books, diplomas, awards, and the like. A prime example of Steinbeck ephemera is his "Pigasus" stamp, currently in the possession of Mrs. Elaine Steinbeck.

Materials About Steinbeck

Any serious Steinbeck collector should not overlook the value of secondary materials *about* him, some of which are out of print and very difficult to find. For example, consider the biographical works of such well-known scholars as Warren G. French, Peter Lisca, Richard Astro, and Jackson J. Benson. There is a large body of literary criticism in the books of Joseph Fontenrose, Howard Levant, F.W. Watt, and others. Critical essays can be found in the literary journals, and there are critical editions of Steinbeck's works, textbooks, and study guides such as those issued by Monarch Press, Coles (Canadian), and Cliff's Notes, which provide basic material for a better understanding of Steinbeck's work. The collector should also be aware that there are several anecdotal works of value, such as *The Wrath of John Steinbeck* (1939) by Robert Bennett and several issues of *John Steinbeck: Personal and Bibliographic Notes* (1939) by Lewis Gannett. In addition there is developing an expanding reference literature about Steinbeck (see pp. 185–194), some of which is very collectible. For example, there are excellent bibliographic sources, such as the Goldstone/Payne bibliography and others by Tetsumaro Hayashi. Professor Hayashi has also produced several study guides and a dictionary of Steinbeck's fictional characters. The latter book is now out of print and a good collectible item.

The list could go on and on, but it does point out one very important thing: It is possible to collect Steinbeckiana in many different areas. Chapter 2 will demonstrate that many different price ranges—some quite reasonable—also exist. Chapter 3 will discuss where to go and how to go about your collecting.

2. The Cost of Steinbeck Collecting

In these times of economic uncertainty almost everyone is concerned about getting the most for his or her money. This is undoubtedly true for book collectors as well. With this in mind, what follows is a rather frank discussion about the current price structure of Steinbeck materials and the problems and frustrations you will more than likely encounter in attempting to purchase them.

Factors Affecting Prices

The antiquarian book field represents a true marketplace. A book, letter, or periodical is worth what someone will pay for it. It is a widely fluctuating market, however, and prices can vary over a wide range for the same piece of material during the same year.[1]

Of the factors that affect the prices of collectible materials, probably the most prominent is *demand*. A book can be rare or very scarce and in pristine condition, but if there is no demand for it, the price will be relatively low. Like the antiquarian market as a whole, demand can also be a highly fluctuating variable, particularly with respect to the works of well-known authors. Some authors seem to fade in and out of popularity, while others remain constantly in the limelight. John Steinbeck seems to fit into this latter category. In fact, there appears to have been a steady increase in the demand for his works over the past two decades. A glance at the current edition of *Books in Print* reveals that many of his major literary works are still in print, especially in paperback editions.

Serving as an adjunct to demand is *availability*. If a book is rare or scarce and is in demand, obviously it will command an inordinately high price on the antiquarian book market. By the same token, if a book is common or in plentiful supply, even though it may be in demand, it will command a much lower price in most instances.

Another major influence upon prices is *condition*. Many collectors feel that condition isn't everything—it's the only thing. This Lombardian philosophy appears to be right on target. There are booksellers who will testify that a collector will pay two or perhaps even three times the normal amount for an absolutely mint copy of a book. Collectors of first editions are particularly hard to please. If it were possible, they would have each of their first editions as new as when it first appeared on the bookstore shelf. Most serious collectors will pay high prices for such copies. Of course, the reverse is also true. A book in poor condition usually will not sell well. Only if a book is rare and there is a demand for it will it have some value despite its poor condition—but at a fraction of what it would be worth in a good to mint state.

Somewhat related to condition is the presence of the original dust jacket. It has been estimated that a dust jacket, even on a recently published book, increases a book's value approximately fifty percent. On books twenty or more years old, especially first editions, the average increase in value nears one hundred percent if the dust jacket is at least in fine condition.[2]

Naturally, prices for antiquarian books are also affected greatly by authors' signatures or inscriptions. These generally can be divided into three categories—limited signed editions, signed trade editions, and association copies. Limited signed editions are normally issued prior to or at the same time as the regular trade edition. They usually maintain a value that is about four to five times the value of the regular first trade edition. Signed trade editions are simply copies of the regular first edition signed or inscribed by the author. If the original recipient of the book is not well known or of any general interest, collectors seem to prefer just the author's name rather than a signed inscription. Usually these signed copies will sell for two to four times the normal price of the book without the autograph. Autographs in later printings of a book will normally increase its value to approximately the level of the first unsigned trade edition, although here, values tend to fluctuate enormously. Association copies are signed books that include an inscription by the author or another famous personality or someone important within the framework of the particular author's writing. These copies will be valued more highly than the normal signed first trade editions, depending on the importance of the recipient involved.[3]

Market Values

Now that you have a general idea of what major factors affect the prices of antiquarian books, let us take a look at the market values of

Steinbeck materials and attempt to understand (if possible) what now exists and what the possible trends might be in the future.

How does a bookseller price a book? This procedure usually involves analyzing the book in terms of several marketing criteria: subject, author, edition, demand, specific clientele, condition of the book, and so on. If the book is well known, the bookseller may consult various reference sources to find out what features make the book interesting to potential buyers. The bookseller may also consult auction records, book catalogs of other dealers, various bibliographies, etc. If the book in question sold for fifty dollars in 1980, the bookseller may extrapolate according to what he or she considers the rate of appreciation in this field, or with this author, and price the book at, say, seventy-five, or a hundred, or perhaps a hundred and fifty dollars. Here, the bookseller will probably be influenced by his or her knowledge of his or her clientele—their interests, buying habits, and so on.[4]

Obviously this type of pricing structure is all very haphazard and highly subjective. After scanning booksellers' catalogs over the past twenty years, this author is convinced that there is absolutely no set of standard guidelines for pricing fine literary property. This is especially true for Steinbeck materials, prices for which, in this era of space travel and exploration, are going into orbit. Given the factors discussed earlier, we can properly assume that John Steinbeck materials have a great deal of popularity in the United States and abroad. Steinbeck's writing, on almost all levels, is in great demand, with some of his scarcer titles commanding extremely high prices.

Holographic materials head the list. For example, a single letter written by Steinbeck to almost anyone will cost around $1,750 or higher. Manuscripts, if they can be found, cost thousands of dollars more.

When considering printed or published materials, galley proofs or proof copies seem to command the highest prices. A good example is Steinbeck's own personal reference set of uncorrected long galleys of *The Grapes of Wrath* (1939) that went recently for $10,000. Prices for these materials usually range from $3,000 to $5,000, depending upon the bookseller. Even a rare saleman's dummy of a Steinbeck title recently sold for $3,500.

In scanning a variety of bookseller's catalogs, *The Bookman's Price Index, American Book Prices Current*, and three editions of Van Allen Bradley's *The Book Collector's Handbook of Values*, I have discovered that over the past five years the average cost of a Steinbeck first trade edition, in fine or near-mint condition, has increased over 52 percent. Limited signed or inscribed editions are almost double that figure.

Another factor affecting the market value of Steinbeck collectible editions is *scarcity*. Several valuable editions are becoming extremely difficult to find, such as the pamphlet *The First Watch*, published in 1947.

An interesting phenomenon in the realm of Steinbeck collecting is the prices of paperback editions. Even though they are more readily available at reasonable cost, some now command prices far beyond their original cost. A good example is the Avon Books No. 77 edition of *The Long Valley*, which originally sold for 25¢; it will now cost you, depending on condition, around $20 to $40. On the average, a paperback first edition in fine to near-mint condition will cost from $10 to $20. Some in poor to good condition will go for around $2 to $5.

3. Guidelines for Productive Steinbeck Collecting

In the preceding chapters you have been introduced to the kinds of Steinbeck materials that are considered to be collectible and some of the problems you can expect to encounter in purchasing these materials. We next turn to the area of sources for Steinbeckiana and methods for making your search more productive.

Of one thing I am quite certain: Haphazard collecting is both unproductive and a waste of your good time. Developing clear goals and objectives in your search for Steinbeck materials is essential if you are to be successful. It will be well worth your time to sit down with pen and paper and write down your plans, always keeping in mind that circumstances change; consequently any goals or objectives you set should be flexible to accommodate any changes that might occur, especially those that relate to your bank account.

Decide, first of all, *what* it is that you want to collect. For instance, if your goal is to collect Steinbeck first editions, your approach will be very different from that of just attempting to fill out your collection with the more commonly available editions. Also, if your bank account is (like mine) not always plush, you might have to engage in considerable long-range planning and saving before you seek out Steinbeck limited or signed editions. More than likely you will have to start with paperback editions and work your way up to the more expensive items. Perhaps you may also be limited by geographical location. If, for example, you live out in the country, your access to many sources is automatically limited, whereas those of us who live in urban areas have close access to many acquisition points. In this case you may have to rely heavily upon the mails.

For beginners who are not precisely certain about what's out there with regard to Steinbeck materials, Tetsumaro Hayashi's two-volume *New Steinbeck Bibliography* (1929–1981) has been published by the Scarecrow Press, Metuchen, New Jersey (1973, 1983). You may also wish to consult the Goldstone/Payne bibliography (now out of print) in a local library. These bibliographies are good sources for compiling "want-lists" of secondary and miscellaneous additions to a growing Steinbeck collection. For currently published materials you will find scanning issues of the *Steinbeck Quarterly* productive.[1]

Once you have decided what types of Steinbeck materials you want to collect, it will be quite useful for you to keep a record of desired items on 3″ × 5″ file cards that will easily fit into pocket or purse. Below is an example:

Want File

Steinbeck, John
Of Mice and Men. New York: Bantam Books, 1955.

These cards can serve as your official "want-list" as you search for materials. When you find an edition, make the following notation on the same card and place it in a separate file:

Steinbeck, John
Of Mice and Men. New York: Bantam Books, 1955.

First edition: Fine Copy
Front wrapper slightly worn.
House of Books, Inc.
6/10/84 – $7.50

This file will assist you in avoiding duplication as your collection grows.

Records such as this can also prove very useful later on if you decide to trade or sell your copy. In addition, they can assist in assessing the fair market value of your collection if the need should arise.

Sources

Local Booksellers

Once your want-list is prepared, the most practical way to begin collecting is to investigate those sources most immediately available to you. This can be accomplished easily by consulting the yellow pages of the telephone book to locate all local used bookshops and secondhand stores. In the process of repeated visits, and with a little luck, you can possibly locate the most common hardbound and paperback editions of Steinbeck's works.[3]

As you visit bookshops, make a special effort to get acquainted with the people who work there, particularly the proprietor. Inform these individuals about your Steinbeck collecting interests and provide them with a copy of your want-list. Many booksellers will hold books aside for you. Some also maintain a card file of their customers and will contact them when certain titles are received in stock. You will be able to learn a great deal about the antiquarian book trade from these booksellers, especially if you listen attentively while in their presence. If on vacation or business trips you have the opportunity to visit other cities, be sure to explore any secondhand or antiquarian bookstores that might carry Steinbeck materials. Many long-sought-after Steinbeck editions have been turned up by traveling book collectors.[4]

Antiquarian Book Fairs

Several times during the year, your local newspaper will carry a notice of an antiquarian book fair. They are usually sponsored by regional branches of the Antiquarian Booksellers Association of America (ABAA) and are held in various sections of the United States. The large regional book fairs often attract booksellers from European countries. Similar fairs of a smaller nature are sometimes sponsored by universities or local clubs. These book fairs are great sources for Steinbeck materials.

Library Book Sales

You will find that many libraries offer book sales once or twice a year in order to raise funds with which to purchase new books or equipment. The books, periodicals, records and the like offered for sale are usually donated by local residents. Prices for materials sold at these events are quite minimal. (As a rule of thumb, be sure to arrive early to get the best bargains.) I have found such sales particularly helpful in locating Steinbeck paperback editions, Reader's Digest Condensed Books, anthologies, and periodicals with Steinbeck short stories and essays. Also, public or academic libraries periodically offer discarded volumes for sale at inexpensive prices. These, however, are usually sold in lots and are picked up by antiquarian booksellers who can more conveniently handle a large number of books at one time. Chances of finding Steinbeck items in these sales are not the best.

Garage Sales

One of the most prevalent local sources for secondhand books in America is the garage sale. Many garage sales offer some books along with other merchandise, but it will save you time and money to respond only to those which specifically indicate books as being included in the sale. If a telephone number is given with the ad, it will be worth your time to phone in advance. Garage sale ads frequently appear in those free advertising weeklies so common today, as well as in local newspapers. Particularly on weekends, you will notice many handmade signs in front of local residences or on corners advertising garage sales. As numerous as they are, garage sales will normally be marginally productive when looking for Steinbeck items, unless you have lots of time on your hands.

Thrift Shops

In your community there is undoubtedly at least one. These establishments are usually operated by churches or charitable organizations such as the Salvation Army or Goodwill. They offer some opportunity for occasional finds of collectible Steinbeck editions at inexpensive prices. As a general rule, you will probably have to scan your way through many shelves of run-of-the-mill materials before you find anything of value (if at all). Thrift stores are most useful for finding Steinbeck short stories in one of the many anthologies in which they have appeared. You may also find some paperback collectible editions on rare occasions. Check the yellow pages for thrift shops in your area and visit them periodically, as they are continually receiving new books and are picked over frequently by local booksellers looking for bargains.

Bazaars and Rummage Sales

Sources closely related to thrift stores are church and charitable bazaars and rummage sales. These fund-raising sales offer an occasional opportunity to find interesting Steinbeck editions at cheap prices. All merchandise is usually donated by local individuals; thus you just might find a very collectible Steinbeck edition if you are lucky. If a phone number is given, be sure to check in advance to see if books are among the items being offered for sale.

Antique Shops

Do not overlook antique shops as you consider various local sources for Steinbeck collectible editions. Most of these establishments carry some supply of secondhand books worthy of investigation. Occasionally a truly collectible Steinbeck edition can be found among them, many times at reasonable prices.

Secondhand Furniture Stores

Used or secondhand furniture dealers must, at times, take lots of books they do not particularly want when purchasing household furnishings for resale. Books in these stores can generally be acquired inexpensively in lots that may contain some Steinbeck items; however, you will probably wind up with much marginal material as well.

Flea Markets

If you have some time on a weekend, a possible great source, particularly of paperback Steinbeck titles, is the local flea market. It may take awhile to discover who has what, but you will find that many exhibitors also sell books. Remember that the early birds in these instances are the only ones who get the good bargains. Also cover the exhibitors several times during the day, since some leave and others arrive all the time.

Estate Sales and Auctions

Scan your local newspaper classified advertisements for upcoming estate sales and auctions. These are normally held on weekends and can be an excellent source for Steinbeck materials at very inexpensive prices. The only problem here is that you often have to carry home many books in order to find a few Steinbeck items if any at all. This is because books are usually auctioned by the boxful or in sets. As usual, it is advisable to arrive at these sales or auctions as early as possible. In the cases of estate sales, you will then get first pick of the items offered. At auctions you can look over the offerings beforehand and take note of those lot numbers that contain Steinbeck items of interest to you. Estate sales and auctions are good places to find Steinbeck editions or books about him that have been stored in attics or basements for a long time.[5]

Rare Book Auctions

Depending on the area in which you live, you might have the opportunity to attend a rare book auction. These auctions are where you might find some of the more difficult-to-locate Steinbeck editions; however, you should be aware that auctions of this nature are attended by the more experienced collectors and booksellers. The major auction houses in the United States are located in New York City. The best known are Sotheby Parke Bernet, Swann Galleries, and Christie's. For those living in the western United States there are the California Book Auction Galleries in San Francisco and Los Angeles. Catalogs are prepared and sold to interested collectors, dealers and librarians.

Newspaper Ads

Get into the habit of scanning the classified ads appearing in your local newspaper, especially on weekends, under any categories that might list books for sale. Along with garage sales these usually will include household items, antiques, miscellaneous and thrifty ads. Also scan the listings in any free weekly newspapers and advertising publications that may be available in your immediate area.

Booksellers' Catalogs

Many booksellers throughout the world issue (with varying degrees of regularity) catalogs offering Steinbeck materials. Some of these dealers may not actually have separate business premises, but will instead use a portion of their private residences in which to engage in a mail-order business. It is possible that at times they will allow admittance to the public, but usually by appointment only. As a Steinbeck collector it will be well worth your while to receive catalogs from as many booksellers as possible, especially those specializing in Steinbeck materials. Check your local public or institutional library for reference books which list antiquarian dealers and their specialties in the United States, Canada, and Great Britain. (Appendix A of this guide will also provide you with a basic list of these booksellers.) Then contact the appropriate booksellers and ask to be put on their mailing lists for future catalogs.

There are several directory-type reference sources that you might find helpful. One is the *Directory of American Book Specialists*, New York: Continental Publishing Company (request most current edition), 1261 Broadway, New York, N.Y. 10001. Another is the *Directory of Specialized American Bookdealers*, New York: Moretus Press, Inc. (1984), 274 Madison Avenue, New York, N.Y. 10016. A specialized periodical, *The Steinbeck Collector*, contains in each issue a list of the major Steinbeck booksellers in the United States. This publication is available from The Bibliographic Research Library, 964 Chapel Hill Way, San Jose, California 95122.

You will also find that booksellers often advertise new catalogs in *A B Bookman's Weekly* (the principal journal of the antiquarian book world), P.O. Box AB, Clifton, New Jersey 07015 and in other publications such as the *New York Times Book Review* and various collectors' magazines. Annually, *A B Bookman's Weekly* issues a yearbook containing listings of booksellers arranged by their specialties, including John Steinbeck.[6]

Antiquarian booksellers use many abbreviations in their catalogs; you can consult Appendix B for the most commonly used ones. Generally you will find it useful to become familiar with book-trade terminology. Also, it is good practice to submit your want-lists to several antiquarian booksellers so that they can quote you a needed Steinbeck edition should they run across one sometime in the future. Remember that it is important, when buying from a bookseller's catalog, to *send in your order promptly*. It is almost a sure bet that someone else out there is looking for the same Steinbeck edition that you are.

After getting your feet wet in the waters of Steinbeck collecting, you may want to become acquainted, and perhaps associate, with others doing the same thing. A good way to start is to get yourself listed in the *International Book Collectors Directory*. (This is available for $35.00 from Pegasus Press, P.O. Box 1350, Vashou Island, Washington 98070.) By so doing you will most likely receive mail from other collectors and possibly from societies or clubs. In a relatively short time you will get to know some of the other Steinbeck collectors in your area. You might also consider joining the John Steinbeck Society of America, for a very nominal membership fee, which will give you access to the largest group of Steinbeck enthusiasts in existence. To get information on this organization, write to the John Steinbeck Society of America, c/o English Department, Ball State University, Muncie, Indiana 47306. The society also has a membership directory that you may purchase for $30.00. After you become acquainted with some of these Steinbeck collectors, make a list of the titles you would like to acquire and send them copies of the list, asking for possible exchanges or direct purchases.

Do not overlook the advantages of personal advertising. A short advertisement stating the particular books that you want (in this case books by and about John Steinbeck) can often be quite effective. These ads can be placed in local newspapers, advertising weeklies, or in collectors' magazines.

Also, you may discover Steinbeck editions within your own family or friends. Inform these people of your interest in John Steinbeck, and you will be surprised how quickly the word can spread.

If you have not done so already, familiarize yourself with the public and institutional libraries in your community and accessible geographic area. In them you will find a good deal of useful information. Books by and about Steinbeck of which you had no previous knowledge can be found in a variety of bibliographic works as well as in the bibliographies of related works. In most large libraries you will find the *National Union Catalog*, published by the Library of Congress, which lists books held by major libraries throughout the United States. The local library can many times prove to be an exhilarating and adventurous place for the avid book collector. It may very well turn out to be a gold mine in your hunt for Steinbeck materials.[7]

A final note: As you have undoubtedly noticed, the main thrust of this guide has been toward the identification and acquisition of Steinbeck materials. Relatively little has been said concerning buying and selling these materials for profit. This omission is by design. If your intended purpose in collecting Steinbeck materials is for profit, many of the works cited in the annotated bibliography will be of value to you. The basic purpose of this guide, however, is to assist those who recognize the literary genius of John Steinbeck and want to obtain editions of his works so that they may gain a deeper understanding of his universal message.

II. Collectible Steinbeck Editions

4. Descriptive Alphabetical List of Steinbeck Editions

The publishing industry in the United States, as well as in many other countries, is big business. As such it is highly individualistic and diversified. Publishers practice individualism by employing their own styles, traditions, and idiocyncrasies in the publications they produce. Consequently there is little uniformity in the practices of these companies in identifying their first or other collectible editions. In many cases, it is simply not possible to determine the edition status of a publication without a reference source of some kind that provides adequate descriptive information.[1]

Dating from the early part of this century, a number of specialists have attempted to provide reference tools that would identify publishers' first editions by listing standard markings and/or listing the main variances in these publications. Several of the more well-known of these guides include Henry S. Boutell's *First Editions of Today and How to Tell Them*, 4th edition (1964); Van Allen Bradley's *The Book Collector's Handbook of Values*, 4th edition (1982); *First Printings of American Authors...*, Edited by Matthew J. Bruccoli and C.E. Frazer Clark, Jr., 4 volumes (1977–1979); William M. McBride's *A Pocket Guide to the Identification of First Editions*, 2d edition (1982), and his additional guide entitled *Points of Issue* (1982); Jack Tannen's *How to Identify and Collect American First Editions...*(1976); and Edward N. Zempel's *A First Edition?* (1977).

In some cases these compendia are adequate in terms of their intended purpose. Overall, however, they simply do not provide the detail necessary for one to determine the edition status of a book. When considering the collectible editions of an important author such as John Steinbeck, there are too many variances in such things as typefaces, decorations, bindings, and the like to be able to authoritatively identify a specific edition. What is needed, therefore, is a reference tool that will provide enough descriptive information that covers all of the variances in specific editions of a book. This kind of tool is more commonly known as a *descriptive bibliography*. Descriptive bibliographies provide full physical descriptions of the books they list, enabling us to tell one edition from another and to identify significant variations within a single edition. Good descriptive bibliographies are therefore indispensable to book collectors, whatever their fields of interest and whatever the time period their collections cover.[2]

Descriptive bibliography of John Steinbeck's works was both too slow and too incomplete to be of much value to book collectors up to 1974. As early as 1936, William J. Henneman appended a brief descriptive bibliography of five Steinbeck titles to an article by Ben Abramson.[3] Almost a year later, Lawrence Clark Powell provided some additional information on various Steinbeck titles published to that time in a bibliographical article.[4] In 1939, Harry T. Moore provided a bibliographical checklist of first editions at the conclusion of his pioneering critical study of Steinbeck's early novels.[5] This brief descriptive checklist includes both book-length works and a few shorter pieces appearing in some anthologies.

No bibliography of a descriptive nature was published after 1939 until the appearance in 1963 of an exhibition catalog of Steinbeck's works contained in the collection of the Humanities Research Center at the University of Texas at Austin.[6] This catalog includes much bibliographical information on thirty-six of Steinbeck's major works published through 1962, including foreign language editions. The next important Steinbeck bibliography was Tetsumaro Hayashi's *John Steinbeck: A Concise Bibliography, 1930–65* (1967).[7] This work did little to assist book collectors in identifying specific standard editions, but it did, for the first time, assemble Steinbeck's literary canon into a useful classification scheme.

In 1974, the Goldstone/Payne bibliography was issued by the Humanities Research Center at the University of Texas.[8] With the publication of this monumental work, the Steinbeck collector now had an extensive and authoritative source for descriptive bibliographic information and could identify, with confidence, many of the Steinbeck collectible editions. This bibliography also included Steinbeck's periodical contributions, contributions to books, foreign language editions, secondary works and the like.

In 1978, this bibliographer authored a small guide to Steinbeck first editions in a pocket-sized format so that collectors would have a source that could easily be carried into bookstores and other places for ready reference.[9] This bibliography was followed in 1979 by a guide to the Steinbeck collection of the Salinas Public Library, compiled by John Gross and Lee Richard Hayman.[10] This work does contain some descriptive data on some Steinbeck editions, but is not as extensive as Goldstone/Payne. It does, however, provide cross-references to Goldstone/Payne.

Another important bibliography was published in 1980. In this year, Bradford Morrow Bookseller, Ltd., issued his Sales Catalogue Eight comprising the Harry Valentine collection.[11] This catalogue provides additional bibliographical information on many Steinbeck editions not covered in the other previously mentioned bibliographies. Also in 1980, the Stanford University Libraries published a catalog of their John Steinbeck collection compiled and edited by Susan F. Riggs.[12] This bibliography is of marginal use to collectors because it does not include much descriptive information on various editions, but it does give some idea of certain editions which are now out of circulation, as does the Salinas Public Library's guide.

Despite this rather extensive bibliographic coverage (especially since 1967), the serious Steinbeck collector is still faced with some difficult problems in identifying and finding various editions as yet not discovered or described. This problem is further exacerbated by the many fugitive editions of Steinbeck titles which continue to elude bibliographers in spite of their unremitting efforts to ferret them out and record them. The alphabetical list below is an attempt to update the current state of Steinbeck editions and what is known about them.

The list is arranged in alphabetical order by title, which will assist the collector in quickly finding information on the edition in hand. The editions of each title are then arranged in chronological sequence. Those editions of a specific title for which the date of publication could not be determined have by necessity been placed at the end of the other editions published in the same year.

Information on each edition includes the imprint data (i.e., place of publication, publisher, and date of publication); number of pages (if available); and additional descriptive information, such as the edition statement, as much physical data as is available, the original price (if available), a current price range, an availability statement, and the source or sources from which the information was obtained.

The price ranges were mostly determined by examining booksellers' catalogs and several bibliographic tools such as *American Book Prices Current*. For those editions not covered in these sources, price ranges were based on this author's expertise as a Steinbeck collector over the past ten years.

Sources used for compiling this list consist of major Steinbeck bibliographies, several universal and national bibliographies, some trade bibliographies, several major publishers, and the collections of several libraries. Below is a key to abbreviations used.

BBIP—*British Books in Print*
BIP—*Books in Print* (United States)
BM—Bradford Morrow (Catalogue Eight)
BNB—*British National Bibliography*
BRL—Bibliographic Research Library
Bantam—Bantam Books
Brit. Mus.—British Museum Catalogue
CBI—*Cumulative Book Index* (United States)
EC—*English Catalogue*
GP—Goldstone/Payne Bibliography
MB—Mitchell Books (Catalog Six)
NUC—*National Union Catalog* (United States)
RC—*Reference Catalogue* (United Kingdom)
SRC—Steinbeck Research Center (San Jose State University—United States)
Viking—The Viking Press
WCBL—*Whittakers Cumulative Book List* (United Kingdom)

For full bibliographic information and annotations see the annotated bibliography.

Great care has been exercised in preparing the descriptions below to make them as accurate as possible, given the eternal presence of human error. The author has examined firsthand all those editions bearing the abbreviations *SRC* and *BRL* as sources or references. All other entries are based on information from the sources indicated and I cannot certify their accuracy.

List of Editions

1. *The Acts of King Arthur and His Noble Knights* (1976) [Malory, Sir Thomas]

a. New York: Farrar, Straus and Giroux, [1976]. 363p.
(First Edition) From the Winchester MSS. of Sir Thomas Malory and other sources edited by Chase Horton. Bound in rough maroon cloth. Blind-stamped on the front cover are two ornamental bands, one on top and one at the bottom within double rules. Has olive green endpapers with top edges stained orange and all edges trimmed. Has a colorful printed dust jacket with a knight design. The back has a photograph of Elaine and John Steinbeck taken at Wells Cathedral, Somerset, England in 1959. Jacket

design by Honi Werner. Published on October 22, 1976 in an edition of 20,000 copies. Originally priced at $10 with current price range estimated at between $10 and $25. Copies of this edition are still relatively easy to obtain. *References:* BM-285, CBI, NUC, SRC, BRL.

b. London: William Heinemann Ltd., [1976] 364p.
(First British Edition) Not seen. Originally priced at £6.50 with current price range estimated at between $15 and $20. Copies of this edition are still relatively easy to obtain. *References:* BM-286, BNB, CBI.

c. New York: Farrar, Straus and Giroux, [1977]. 363p.
(Paperback Edition) Not seen. Has wrappers which reproduce the same design as on the dust jacket of the hardbound edition. Original price is unknown. Current price range is estimated at between $5 and $10. Availability of this edition is unknown. *Reference:* BM-287.

d. New York: Ballantine Books, [1977]. 451p.
(First Ballantine Paperback Edition: Del Rey Books) This edition adds new cover art by Darrell Sweet. Published in November of 1977. Originally priced at $2.50 with a current price range estimated at between $5 and $10. Copies of this edition are still relatively easy to obtain. *References:* BM-288, BIP, BRL.

e. London: Pan Books, 1979. 366p.
(Pan Books Paperback Edition) Not seen. Originally priced at £1.00 with a current price range estimated at between $5 and $10. Copies of this edition are still relatively easy to obtain. *References:* BNB, BBIP.

f. New York: Ballantine Books, 1980. 451p.
(Second Ballantine Paperback Edition: Del Rey Books) Originally priced at $2.95 with a current price range estimated at between $5 and $10. Copies of this edition are still relatively easy to obtain. *References:* CBI, BIP.

g. New York: Avenel Books, [1982]. 363p.
(Reprint Hardbound Edition) Has same dust jacket as first edition except that the photo of John and Elaine Steinback on the back is replaced by a repetition of the front cover and the publisher is printed on the lower part of the spine. Bound in a burnt orange

imitation cloth with dark blue printing on the spine. All edges are trimmed. Originally priced at $10, with a current price range estimated at between $7 and $15. Copies of this reprint edition are common. *Reference:* BRL.

2. *America and Americans* (1966)

a. New York: The Viking Press, [1966]. 207p.
(First Edition) Text by John Steinbeck. Photographs edited by the staff of Studio Books, The Viking Press. Bound in half-green and half-blue cloth covering the spine in blue. Lettering on the spine is stamped in gold. All edges are unstained and untrimmed. Both front and back endpapers are decorated with a map of the United States. Issued in a blue, green and white dust jacket printed in black. Jacket design by Christopher Harris. Also issued in a gray paperboard case. Published on October 12, 1966. Selections first appeared in *The Saturday Evening Post*, July 2, 1966. A binding variant has been noted with the spine reading vertically from the bottom to the top. Originally priced at $12.50 with current price range estimated at between $25 and $75. Copies of this edition are still relatively easy to obtain. *References:* GP-A43a, BM-271–272, CBI, NUC, SRC, BRL.

b. London: William Heinemann Ltd., [1966]. 207p.
(First British Edition) Not seen. Bound in blue cloth. Lettering on spine is stamped in gold. Top edges stained blue and all edges trimmed. The endpapers are decorated with a map of the United States. Issued in a blue, green, and white dust jacket printed in black. Published in October of 1966. Originally priced at £5.10 with current price range estimated at between $20 and $50. Copies of this edition appear to be rather difficult to find. *References:* GP-A43b, BNB, BBIP, CBI.

c. Toronto: Macmillan, 1966. 207p.
(First Canadian Edition) Not seen. Published at the same time as the Viking Press edition. Originally priced at $15.50 with a current price range estimated at between $20 and $50. Copies of this edition appear to be rather difficult to find. *References:* GP-A43c, CBI.

d. New York: Bonanza Books, [1966]. 207p.
(Reprint Edition) A reprint of the Viking Press first edition with

some changes on the recto and verso of the title page. Bound in white cloth extending onto the front and back covers. Lettering on the spine is stamped in black. There is no map of the United States printed on the front endpapers; however, there is one on the back. The paper stock is lighter than that used in the Viking Press edition. Original price is unknown. The current price range is estimated at between $10 and $20. Copies of this edition appear to be rather difficult to find. *References:* SRC, BRL.

e. New York: The Viking Press, 1966. 207p.
(Book-of-the-Month Club Edition) Not seen. Published in December of 1966. Original Club price unknown. The current price range is estimated at between $10 and $20. Copies of this edition surprisingly appear to be rather difficult to locate. *Reference:* GP-A43d.

f. New York: Bantam Books, [1968]. 221p.
(First Bantam Books Paperback Edition, No. Q 3811) Published in October of 1968. The front cover photograph is by Milton E. Stiles. Originally priced at $1.25 with current price range estimated at between $5 and $10. Copies of this edition are still relatively easy to obtain. *References:* GP-A43e, BM-273, CBI, SRC, BRL.

3. *Bombs Away, The Story of a Bomber Team* (1942)

a. New York: The Viking Press, 1942. 185p.
(First Edition) Written for the U.S. Army Air Forces by John Steinbeck with 60 photographs by John Swope. Bound in blue cloth. Front cover has a figure of a plane wing, stars and clouds stamped in black and white. Lettering and designs on the spine are printed in black and white. The dust jacket has the figure of a plane wing and clouds printed in blue, yellow, and black. Jacket design by Arthur Hawkins, Jr. Published on November 27, 1942. Originally priced at $2.50 with current price range estimated at between $50 and $175. Copies of this edition are still relatively easy to obtain. *References:* GP-A18a, BM-161, CBI, SRC, BRL.

b. Toronto: Macmillan, [1942]. 185p.
(First Canadian Edition) Not seen. Published at the same time as the Viking Press edition. Originally priced at $3.25 with current price range estimated at between $25 and $75. Copies of this edition are very difficult to locate. *References:* GP-A18b, CBI.

c. New York: Harper & Brothers, 1942. ?p.
(School Edition) Not seen. Intended for use in the classroom. The title page is different from the Viking Press edition stating: "School Edition Published by Harper & Brothers by arrangement with New York The Viking Press 1942." The text is reprinted from the first edition plates and the sheets are bound in a coarse black cloth stamped in yellow down the spine: "Bombs Away John Steinbeck School Edition Harper." Original price unknown. The current price range is estimated between $200 and $350. Copies of this edition appear to be extremely difficult to find. *Reference:* BM-163.

4. *Burning Bright, a Play in Story Form—Novel* (1950)

a. New York: The Viking Press, 1950. 159p.
(First Edition) Bound in gray cloth. Lettering and design on front cover and spine are stamped in red. Top edges stained orange, all edges trimmed. Issued in a yellow, gray, and orange dust jacket printed in black. A review copy slip in the Goldstone copy gives the publishing date as October 20, 1950. Originally Steinbeck had entitled this play-novel "In the Forests of the Night." Rodgers and Hammerstein [producers of the play], however, thought this title to be a "touch literary" so Steinbeck changed it to *Burning Bright* (see *Steinbeck: A Life in Letters*, pp. 404–405), but not before Viking Press had printed an unknown number of dust jackets with the previous title. These dust jackets are rare and quite expensive. The book originally priced at $2.50 with the current price range estimated at between $20 and $90. Copies of this edition are still relatively easy to obtain. *References:* GP-A29a, BM-206, NUC, CBI, SRC, BRL.

b. Toronto: Macmillan, 1950. 159p.
(First Canadian Edition) Not seen. Published at the same time as the Viking Press edition. Original price unknown. The current price range is estimated to be between $20 and $75. Copies of this edition are difficult to locate. *Reference:* GP-A29c.

c. London: William Heinemann Ltd., [1951]. 111p.
(First British Edition) Not seen. Bound in red cloth. Lettering on spine stamped in gold. Heinemann windmill blind-stamped on the lower right-hand corner of the back cover. All edges unstained and trimmed. Issued in an illustrated dust jacket. Published in August of 1951. Originally priced at 7s. 6d., with current price range

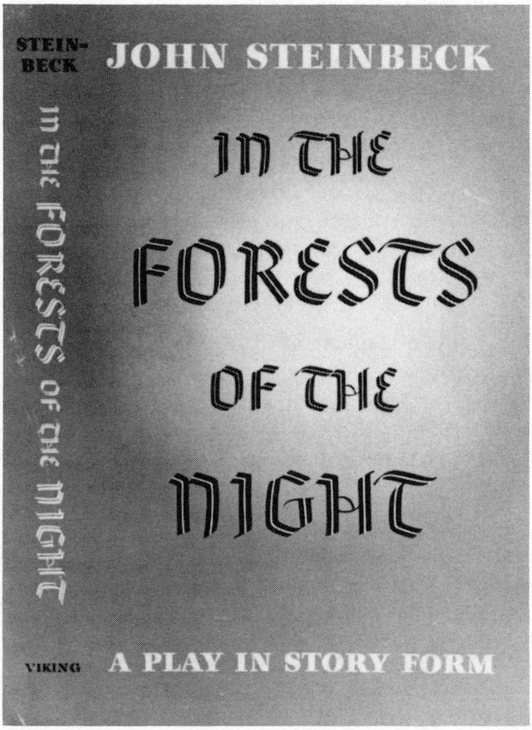

The title was changed to "Burning Bright," but not before Viking Press had printed an unknown number of dust jackets, like the one shown above, with the original title.

estimated at between $50 and $85. Copies of this edition appear to be difficult to find. *References:* GP-A29b, BM-207, BNB, CBI, EC, WCBL.

d. New York: Bantam Books, [1951]. 109p.
(First Bantam Paperback Edition, No. 953) Published in December of 1951. Originally priced at 25¢ with current price range estimated at between $10 and $30. Copies of this edition are apparently becoming more difficult to locate. *References:* GP-A29e, BM-208, BRL.

e. London: Pan Books, [1954]. 160p.
(Pan Paperback Edition, No. 279, combined with *The Pearl*) Not

seen. Published on March 19, 1954. Originally priced at 2s., with current price range estimated at between $10 and $25. Copies of this edition appear to be difficult to find. *References:* GP-A29f, EC, WCBL.

f. London: William Heinemann Ltd., [1967]. 111p.
(A Reissue of the 1951 Edition) Not seen. Originally priced at 21s., with a current price range estimated at between $10 and $50. Copies of this edition appear to be difficult to obtain. *References:* GP-A29g, BNB, EC.

g. London: William Heinemann, Ltd., [1970]. ?p.
(Apparently Another Reissue of the 1951 Edition) Not seen. Original price unknown. The current price range is estimated at between $10 and $50. Copies of this edition except for Goldstone/Payne do not seem to exist. *Reference:* GP-A29h.

h. London: Pan Books, [1970]. 96p.
(Another Pan Paperback Edition) Not seen. Published in September of 1970. Originally priced at £0.20 with current price range estimated at between $5 and $20. Copies of this edition appear to be relatively easy to locate. *Reference:* BBIP.

i. [London]: Heron Books, [1971]. 227p.
(Heron Uniform Edition combined with *The Moon Is Down*) Illustrated by Robert C. Bates. Original price unknown. The current price range is estimated at between $100 and $200. Copies of the edition are very difficult to find. *References:* GP-A29i, CBI, SRC.

j. [Harmondsworth, Eng., New York]: Penguin Books, [1979]. 106p.
(Penguin Paperback Edition) Not seen. Originally priced at $2.95 with current price range estimated between $5 and $10. Copies of this edition are relatively easy to obtain. *References:* CBI, BIP.

5. *Burning Bright; Play in Three Acts—Play* (1951)

[New York]: Dramatists Play Service, [1951]. 56p.
(Paperback Acting Edition) Not seen. Based on the novel with the same name. Bound in wrappers and includes illustrations. Originally priced at 85¢ with current price range estimated at between $5 and $20. Copies of this edition appear to be difficult to obtain. *References:* GP-A29d, NUC, CBI.

6. *Cannery Row* (1945)

a. New York: The Viking Press, 1945. 208p.
(First Edition, Issue in Wrappers) This issue was probably the advance review issue of this novel, bound in blue wrappers and printed in black on the front cover. All edges unstained and untrimmed. Not for sale. The current price range is estimated at between $200 and $550. Copies of this issue of the first edition are extremely difficult to locate. *References:* GP-A22a, BM-173, SRC.

b. New York: The Viking Press, 1945. 208p.
(First Edition, Hardbound Trade Edition) Bound in light buff cloth. Lettering and rules on the front cover and spine are stamped in blue. Top edges stained blue, all edges trimmed. Issued in a colored pictorial dust jacket designed by Arthur Hawkins. Published in January of 1945. There is a variant binding noted of canary-yellow cloth. According to Frederick B. Adams, Jr., who obtained his information from Glick and Colman of The Viking Press, "There was not enough light buff cloth available, so the yellow was selected to finish the run." Originally priced at $2 with current price range estimated at between $75 and $200. Copies of this edition are advertised from time to time but are becoming increasingly difficult to find especially with the light buff binding. *References:* GP-A22b, BM-174, NUC, SRC.

c. Toronto: Macmillan, [1945]. 208p.
(First Canadian Edition) Not seen. Published on the same day as the Viking Press edition. Originally priced at $2.50 with a current price range estimated at between $20 and $50. Copies of this edition are difficult to locate. *References:* GP-A22d, CBI.

d. London: William Heinemann Ltd., [1945]. 136p.
(First British Edition) Not seen. Bound in strong orange-yellow cloth (Centroid 68). Lettering on front cover and spine is stamped in black. The Heinemann windmill is stamped in black horizontally at the base of the spine. All edges are unstained and trimmed. Issued in a blue dust jacket printed in yellow and white. There are two noted binding variants: (1) brilliant orange-yellow cloth (Centroid 67), and (2) deep orange cloth (Centroid 51). Originally priced at 7s. 6d., with current price range estimated at between $100 and $250. Copies of this edition are difficult to find. *References:* GP-A22c, NUC, BM-175, CBI.

e. New York: The Viking Press, [1945]. 208p.
(Book-of-the-Month Club Edition) Bound in light blue cloth. Lettering and rules on the front cover and spine stamped in dark blue and gold. Original subscription price unknown. The current price range is estimated at between $10 and $20. Copies of this edition are still available but appear to be increasingly hard to locate. *References:* GP-A22e, BRL.

f. New York: Council on Books in Wartime, [c1945]. 224p.
(Armed Services Edition, No. T-5) Published in paperback for distribution among military personnel during World War II. Not for sale. The current price range is estimated at between $15 and $40. Copies of this edition are becoming difficult to locate. *References:* GP-A22f, NUC, SRC, BRL.

g. New York: P.F. Collier Corporation, [c1945?]. ?p.
(Collier Uniform Edition) Not seen. Published in the uniform Collier binding of brown cloth with pictorial stamping in blue, maroon, and gold. This edition includes stories from *The Long Valley*. Original price unknown. The current price range is estimated at between $20 and $40. Copies of this edition are difficult to obtain. *References:* GP-A22g, NUC.

h. New York: Book League of America, 1945. ?p.
(Book League of America Edition) Not seen. Published in May of 1945. Original price unknown. The current price range is estimated at between $20 and $75. Copies of this Book League edition are very difficult to locate. *Reference:* Bantam.

i. Garden City, N.Y.: Garden City Publishing Co., 1946. 208p.
(Apparently a Reprint Edition) Not seen. Originally priced at $1, with current price range estimated at between $5 and $15. Copies of this edition are apparently difficult to obtain. *Reference:* CBI.

j. [Toronto]: Blue Ribbon Books, 1946. 208p.
(Apparently a Reprint Edition) Not seen. Originally priced at $1.39, with a current price range estimated at between $5 and $15. Copies of this edition are difficult to locate. *Reference:* CBI.

k. New York: The Sun Dial Press, [1946]. 181p.
(Sun Dial Reprint Edition) Originally priced at $1, with a current price range estimated at between $15 and $25. Copies of this edition

are somewhat difficult to find. *References:* GP-A22h, Bantam, NUC, BRL.

l. New York: Bantam Books, [1947]. 152p.
(First Bantam Paperback Edition, No. 75) Has illustrated end-papers both in front and back. Originally priced at 25¢, with a current price range estimated at between $10 and $25. Copies of this edition are becoming rather difficult to locate. *References:* GP-A22i, NUC, BRL.

m. London: Reprint Society, [1947]. ?p.
(British Reprint Edition) Not seen. Combined with *Of Mice and Men*. Published with the title *Two in One*. Original price unknown. The current price range is estimated at between $10 and $20. Copies of this edition are difficult to obtain. *Reference:* GP-A22j.

n. London: Penguin Books, [1949]. 249p.
(Penguin Paperback Edition, No. 717) Not seen. Combined with *Of Mice and Men*. Published in October of 1949. Originally priced at 1s. 6d., with a current price range estimated at between $5 and $15. Copies of this edition are now relatively difficult to find. *References:* GP-A22k, EC.

o. New York: Bantam Books, [1954]. 123p.
(New Bantam Paperback Edition, No. 1266) Published in September of 1954 with a new cover. Originally priced at 25¢, with a current price range estimated at between $10 and $25. Copies of this edition are relatively difficult to locate. *References:* BM-176, NUC, BRL.

p. New York: Bantam Books, [1959]. 123p.
(Bantam Classic Paperback Edition, No. AC18) Published in February of 1959 with a new cover design. Originally priced at 35¢, with a current price range estimated at between $2 and $4. Copies of this edition are relatively easy to obtain. *References:* BIP, NUC, BRL.

q. New York: The Viking Press, 1963. 181p.
(Completely Reset Hardbound Edition) Issued without a dust jacket. Originally priced at $4, with a current price range estimated at between $5 and $10. Copies of this edition are relatively easy to locate. *References:* GP-A221, BM-179, NUC, BIP, SRC.

r. New York: The Viking Press, [1963]. 181p.
(Compass Book Paperback Edition, No. C131) Issued with a cover design by Arthur Hawkins. Originally priced at $1.45, with a current price range estimated at between $2.50 and $10. Copies of this edition are relatively easy to obtain. *References:* GP-A22m, BM-177, CBI, BIP, BRL.

s. London: William Heinemann Ltd., 1967. 136p.
(Apparently a Reprint of the 1945 Edition) Not seen. Originally priced at 21s., with a current price range estimated at between $5 and $20. Copies of this edition are relatively easy to locate. *References:* GP-A22o, BNB, BBIP, NUC, CBI.

t. New York: Franklin Watts, [1968]. 208p.
(Large Type Edition—"A Keith Jennison Book") Not seen. Goldstone/Payne (A22h) erroneously list the publication date of this edition as 1966, and the Library of Congress is uncertain about the exact date. Apparently the publication date was not made clear by Watts on the verso of the title page. Originally priced at $7.95, with a current price range estimated at between $20 and $40. Copies of this edition are difficult to find. *References:* GP-A22h, NUC, CBI, BIP.

u. [n.p., London]: Heron Books, [1971]. 461p.
(Heron Uniform Edition) Combined with *Sweet Thursday* and illustrated by Peter Whiteman. Original price unknown. The current price range is estimated at between $100 and $200. Copies of this edition are very difficult to find. *References:* GP-A22p, NUC, CBI, SRC.

v. London: Heinemann Educational, 1971. 136p.
(The New Windmill Series, No. 150) Not seen. Goldstone/Payne (A22q) lists also a 1971 Heinemann edition which does not appear bibliographically in any of the British national or trade bibliographies. This edition seems to be a reprint of the 1945 Heinemann edition. Originally priced at £0.40, with a current price range estimated at between $5 and $15. Copies of this edition appear to be difficult to find as are some British editions in the United States. *References:* GP-A22r, BNB, BBIP.

w. London: Pan Books, 1974. 156p.
(First Pan Books Paperback Edition) Not seen. Originally priced at £0.35, with a current price range estimated at between $2 and $5.

Copies of this edition are relatively easy to obtain. *References:* BNB, BBIP.

x. New York: Bantam Books, [1982]. 123p.
(New Bantam Paperback Edition) Front cover depicts a scene from the MGM movie. Originally priced at $2.25. No price range. Still in print. Copies of this edition are very common. *Reference:* BRL.

7. Chapter Thirty-Four from the Novel *East of Eden* (1952)

[Bronxville, N.Y.]: Privately Printed, 1952. [12] unnumbered pages
(First Separate Edition) On page [9] at the end of the text is the following limitation notice printed in red: "125 copies have been printed on the hand-press by Valenti Angelo at Bronxville, New York with the kind permission of John Steinbeck and The Viking Press. [*manuscript*] Valenti Angelo." Bound in limp buff wrappers, with inner folds, reinforced between front and back covers and front and back endpapers with tipped-in white chipboard. Thread inner ties. Lettering and design on front cover printed in black and red. Top edges trimmed, front and bottom edges untrimmed. Three variant copies have been noted for which priority has not been determined: (1) No design on the title page. The limitation notice appears on page [10]. (2) Title page contains a red and black rectangular design of leafy and bare branches between the title and "*PRIVATELY PRINTED 1952*." The limitation notice appears on page [10]. (3) The title on the cover and title page is: [*ornament, oak leaf*] *WHAT IS THE WORLD'S STORY/ ABOUT? FROM THE NOVEL/ EAST OF EDEN BY JOHN STEINBECK*. The circular JS design appears on the title page and the limitation notice is at the bottom of page [9]. Apparently not for sale. The current price range is estimated at between $100 and $250. Copies of this special printing are very difficult to locate. *References:* GP-A32d, NUC, SRC.

8. *The Collected Poems of Amnesia Glasscock* (1976)

South San Francisco, Calif.: ManRoot, 1976. 32p. [unpaged]
Published on July 1, 1976 in a limited edition of two hundred-fifty numbered copies. Handset and printed in Caslon Original Old Style on Antique Laid paper with Curtis covers by Peter Lewis and Clive Matson in Neon Sun. Handsewn in paper wrappers with cover

illustration by Jose Laffitte. Issued in a tissue dust jacket. These poems, once believed to have been written by John Steinbeck, have now been attributed to his first wife, the late Carol Henning Brown. Originally priced at $20; the current price range is estimated at between $40 and $75. Copies of this publication are still relatively easy to locate. *References:* NUC, SRC, BRL (photocopy).

9. *Commencement Program of Salinas Union High School June '19.* (1919)

[Salinas: Salinas Union High School], June 13–16, 1919.
This is the original printed program for the commencement of Steinbeck's senior class. This rare program lists Steinbeck as Senior Class President, and as playing the lead role in the class play—Justin Rawson, in "Mrs. Bumpstead-Leigh" by Harry J. Smith. Comprised of a single leaf folded once to make four pages of text. Not for sale. The current price range is estimated at between $400 and $700. Copies of this publication are very rare. *Reference:* BM-691.

10. *Cup of Gold, A Life of Henry Morgan, Buccaneer, with Occasional Reference to History* (1929)

a. New York: Robert M. McBride & Company, 1929. 269p.
(First Edition, First Issue) Bound in bright yellow cloth. Lettering on both the front cover and the spine is in black. Top edges stained blue and trimmed, front edges untrimmed, bottom edges trimmed. Issued in a rather flamboyant piratical dust jacket. First published in August of 1929. McBride printed 2476 copies, of which 939 were remaindered to one Max Salop of the Harlem Book Company. It is these unbound printed sheets that undoubtedly were purchased by Covici-Friede, who reissued them with new preliminaries, preface, binding, and a dust jacket but with the McBride colophon remaining on the final page of text. Two physical variants have been noted: (1) Copies with the top edges unstained, and (2) Copies with the top edges unstained and lacking the final blank leaf. Originally priced at $2.50, with a current price range estimated at between $55 and $2500. Copies of this first issue are extremely difficult to find and are very expensive depending on condition. *References:* GP-A1a, BM-1, NUC, CBI, SRC.

b. New York: Covici-Friede Publishers, [1936]. 269p.
(First Edition, Second Issue) This issue carries a new preface by Lewis Gannett, and has a different title page. Bound in maroon cloth. Lettering on the spine is stamped in gold. Top edges stained blue, all edges trimmed, issued in a colored dust jacket depicting a woman, several pirates and a ship in the background. The words *COVICI/ FRIEDE* on the spine are blacked over with *COVICI/ FRIEDE* printed above. Originally priced at $2.50, with a current price range estimated at between $200 and $500. Copies of this edition are also extremely difficult to obtain. *References:* GP-A1b, BM-2, NUC, CBI, SRC.

c. New York: Covici-Friede Publishers, [1936]. 269p.
(Second Edition) Bound in dark blue cloth. There are a scroll and ship blind-stamped on the front cover. The lettering and decorations on the spine are stamped in gold. Top edges stained blue, all edges trimmed. Issued in a dust jacket similar to the First Edition, Second Issue except no publisher is printed on the spine and to the front is added: *AUTHOR OF/ "OF MICE AND MEN."* There have been some copies noted with the fore edges untrimmed. Three typographical errors also appear in this edition. On page 211, the last word on the third line up from the bottom "their" is misspelled "theiir." On page 255, in the second word on line 23 "like," the "e" is missing. And on page 259, the first word "I" on line one is indented two spaces when it should be even with the left-hand margin of the text. Originally priced at $2.50, with a current price range estimated at between $35 and $100. Copies of this edition are now becoming difficult to locate. *References:* GP-A1c, BM-3 & 4, NUC, SRC, BRL.

d. London: William Heinemann Ltd., [1937]. 268p.
(First British Edition) Published in January of 1937. Bound in blue cloth. Lettering and rules on the spine are stamped in gold. The Heinemann windmill is blind-stamped on the lower right-hand corner of the back cover. All edges unstained and trimmed. Issued in a printed dust jacket. Originally priced at 7s. 6d., with a current price range estimated at between $900 and $1500. Copies of this edition seem to be very scarce. *References:* GP-A1d, BM-5, NUC, CBI.

e. Toronto: McLeod, [1937]. 277p.
(First Canadian Edition) Not seen. Apparently the original price was $2.50. The current price range is estimated at between $25 and

$75. Copies of this edition are very difficult to find. *References:* GP-A1e, CBI.

f. New York: The Sun Dial Press, 1938. 269p.
(Sun Dial Reprint Edition) Not seen. Originally priced at 79¢, with a price range estimated at between $10 and $30. Copies of this edition appear to be difficult to locate. *References:* GP-A1f, CBI.

g. [New York]: The American Mercury, Inc., [1939]. 126p.
(A Mercury Book Paperback Edition, No. 20) Published with the subtitle: *the Amazing Career of Sir Henry Morgan, Buccaneer, with Occasional Reference to History*. Originally priced at 25¢, with a current price range estimated at between $5 and $15. Copies of this edition are difficult to find. *References:* GP-A1g, BM-6, NUC, CBI, SRC, BRL.

h. New York: P.F. Collier Corporation, [1940]. 269p.
(Collier Uniform Edition) Published in the uniform Collier binding of brown cloth with pictorial stamping in blue, maroon, and gold. Original price unknown. The current price range is estimated at between $20 and $40. Copies of this edition are difficult to obtain. *References:* GP-A1h, BM-7, BRL.

i. Cleveland: World Publishing Company, [1944]. 269p.
(Tower Books Edition) Not seen. Published in February of 1944 with a dust jacket designed by Monroe Reisman which depicts "the king of the free booters" Henry Morgan forcing himself on a terrified female Hollywood-type. Originally priced at 49¢, with a current price range estimated at between $10 and $30. Copies of this edition are still relatively easy to obtain. *References:* GP-A1i, BM-8, NUC, CBI.

j. New York: Council on Books in Wartime, [circa 1945]. 285p.
(Armed Services Edition, 750) Published in paperback for distribution among military personnel during World War II. Not for sale. The current price range is estimated at between $15 and $40. Copies of this edition are becoming difficult to locate. *References:* GP-A1j, BM-9, NUC, SRC, BRL.

k. New York: Popular Library, [c1949]. 191p.
(Popular Library Paperback Edition, No. 216) Issued in pictorial wrappers designed by Rudolph Baring. Originally priced at 25¢, with a current price range estimated at between $10 and $20. Copies

of this edition can still be located but are becoming harder to find. *References:* GP-A1k, BM-10, SRC, BRL, NUC.

l. New York: Bantam Books, [1953]. 198p.
(First Bantam Paperback Edition, No. 1184) Published in December of 1953. Originally priced at 25¢, with a current price range estimated at between $5 and $15. Copies of this edition are still relatively easy to locate. *References:* GP-A1l, BM-11, SRC, BRL.

m. London: Transworld Publishers, [1953]. 212p.
(Corgi Books Paperback Series, No. T6) Not seen. Published on May 20, 1953. Originally priced at 2s., with a current price range estimated at between $5 and $15. Copies of this edition are difficult to locate. *References:* GP-A1m, BM-12, BNB, EC, WcBL.

n. London: William Heinemann Ltd., [1968]. 268p.
(A Reprint of the 1937 Edition) Not seen. Published in December of 1968. Originally priced at 30s., with a current price range estimated at between $10 and $20. Copies of this edition are difficult to obtain. *References:* GP-A1n, BNB, BBIP, CBI.

o. Leicester, Eng.: F.A. Thorpe, 1973. 357p.
(Large Print Edition – Ulverscroft Large Print Series; Fiction) Not seen. Originally priced at £1.50, with a current price range estimated at between $5 and $15. Copies of this edition are relatively easy to locate. *Reference:* BNB.

p. Harmondsworth, Eng., New York: Penguin Books, 1976. 198p.
(First Penguin Paperback Edition) Cover design by Neil Stuart. Originally priced at $1.95, with a current price range estimated at between $3 and $7. Copies of this edition are quite common. *References:* BM-13, NUC, BNB, BRL.

11. *East of Eden* (1952)

a. New York: The Viking Press, 1952. 602p.
(First Edition, Limited Issue) This autographed edition was limited to fifteen hundred copies, seven hundred and fifty of which were for private distribution. Bound in green cloth. Spine stamped in gold on a brown background and enclosed in a gold rule: *JOHN/ STEINBECK/ East/ OF/ Eden/ VIKING*. All edges stained terra-

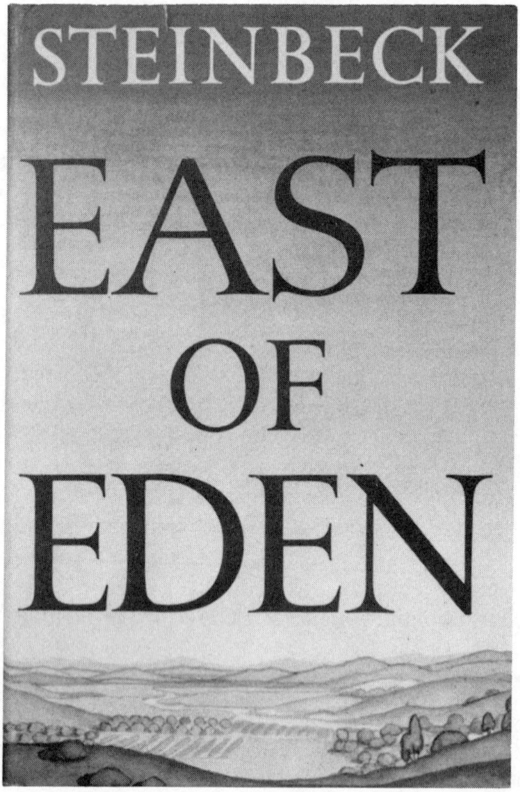

The regular trade first edition (with dust jacket) of "East of Eden."

cotta and trimmed. Issued in a glassine wrapper and a publisher's brown paperboard case. Published in September of 1952. Originally priced at $12.50, with a current price range estimated at between $250 and $475. Copies of this limited issue are now difficult to find. *References:* GP-A32a, BM-217, NUC, CBI, SRC.

b. New York: The Viking Press, 1952. 602p.
(Regular Trade First Edition) Published in September of 1952 in an edition of 110,000 copies. Bound in green cloth. On the front cover printed in dark green is: *East of Eden/ JOHN STEINBECK*. On the spine printed in black on a brown background and enclosed within a rule is: *JOHN/ STEINBECK/ East / OF/ Eden/ VIKING*. Top edges stained yellow, all edges trimmed. Issued in a colored pictorial dust jacket. On page 281, line 38 "bite" for "bight," corrected only in

the Bantam Books edition. Originally priced at $4.50, with a current price range estimated at between $50 and $250. Copies of this edition are still quite common. *References:* GP-A32b, BM-218, NUC, CBI, SRC, BRL.

c. Toronto: Macmillan, 1952. 602p.
(First Canadian Edition) Not seen. Published in September of 1952. Original price unknown. The current price range is estimated at between $75 and $150. Copies of this edition are difficult to find. *Reference:* GP-A32e.

d. London: William Heinemann Ltd., [1952]. 525p.
(First British Edition) Not seen. Published on November 24, 1952. Bound in green cloth. Lettering and rules on the spine are stamped in gold. The Heinemann windmill is blind-stamped on the lower right-hand corner of the back cover. All edges unstained and trimmed. Issued in a blue and yellow dust jacket printed in black and white. Originally priced at 15s., with a current price range estimated at between $100 and $200. Copies of this edition are difficult to locate. *References:* GP-A32c, BM-219, NUC, CBI.

e. New York: The Viking Press, [c1953]. 662p.
(Book-of-the-Month Club Edition) Not seen. Combined with *The Wayward Bus*. Apparently reprinted in 1962. Issued in a dust jacket designed by Al Schmidt. Original subscription price unknown. The current price range is estimated at between $10 and $20. Copies of this edition are difficult to find. *References:* GP-A32g, BM-220, NUC.

f. Chicago: Sears Readers Club, [1953]. 602p.
(Sears Readers Club Edition) Not seen. Published by subscription to members of the Club in July of 1953. Original subscription price unknown. The current price range is estimated at between $20 and $90. Copies of this edition are difficult to obtain. *References:* GP-A32h, BM-221, NUC.

g. New York: Grosset & Dunlap, [1955]. 602p.
(Grosset & Dunlap Reprint Edition) Not seen. Apparently a reprint of the 1952 regular Viking trade edition. Originally priced at $1.98, with a current price range estimated at between $20 and $50. Copies of this edition are difficult to find. *References:* GP-A32i, CBI.

h. New York: Bantam Books, [1955]. 534p.
(First Bantam Paperback Edition, No. F1267) Published in January of 1955, 1st printing in December of 1954. Originally priced at 50¢, with a current price range estimated at between $5 and $15. Copies of this edition appear to be difficult to locate. *References:* GP-A32j, BM-222, BRL.

i. London: World Distributors, [1957]. 573p.
(Viking Books Editions, No., V.S. 503) Not seen. Goldstone/Payne list the publisher as Consul Books, whereas BNB lists World Distributors. Published in paperback in April of 1957. Originally priced at 3s. 6d., with a current price range estimated at between $5 and $10. Copies of this edition are not easy to find. *References:* GP-A32k, BNB, EC.

j. London: Pan Books, [1963]. 568p.
(First Pan Books Paperback Edition) Not seen. Goldstone/Payne lists this edition as being published in 1965. Their copy may have been a later printing. Published on July 5, 1963. Originally priced at 6s., with a current price range estimated at between $5 and $10. Copies of this edition are difficult to find. *References:* GP-A32l, BBIP, WCBL.

k. London: William Heinemann Ltd., [1968]. 525p.
(A Reissue of the 1952 Edition) Not seen. Published in June of 1968. Originally priced at 42s., with a current price range estimated at between $10 and $20. Copies of this edition are difficult to obtain. *References:* BNB, WCBL, NUC, CBI.

l. New York: The Viking Press, [1970]. 602p.
(Apparently a Reissue of the 1952 Trade Edition) Not seen. Originally priced at $7.95, with a current price range estimated at between $10 and $20. Copies of this edition are quite common. *Reference:* GP-A32m.

m. New York: The Viking Press, [1970]. 602p.
(Compass Paperback Edition, No. C278) Not seen. Originally priced at $2.45, with a current price range estimated at between $5 and $15. Copies of this edition are fairly common. *References:* GP-A32n, BM-223, BIP, NUC.

n. [n.p., London]: Distributed by Heron Books, [1971]. 526p.
(Heron Uniform Edition) Contains illustrations by Patricia Ludlow. Issued in a uniform imitation leather binding. Original

price unknown. The current price range is estimated at between $100 and $200. Copies of this edition are very hard to locate. *References:* GP-A32p, NUC, CBI, SRC.

o. Leicester, Eng.: Ulverscroft, 1976. 436p.
(Ulverscroft Large Print Series; Fiction) Not seen. This edition is a condensation by the editors of the Reader's Digest Condensed Books. This condensation was originally published: Pleasantville, N.Y.; London: Reader's Digest Association, 1962. Originally priced at £2.65, with a current price range estimated at between $10 and $15. Copies of this edition are fairly common. *Reference:* BNB.

p. Harmondsworth, Eng., New York: Penguin Books, [1979]. 691p.
(First Penguin Books Edition) Originally priced at £1.25 or $2.95, with a current price range estimated at between $5 and $7. Copies of this edition are quite common. *References:* CBI, BRL.

12. *The First Watch* (1947)

[Los Angeles, Calif.: The Ward Ritchie Press], Christmas, 1947. 6p.
(First and Only Separate Edition) Published in a total edition of 60 numbered copies, 10 of which were for the use of the author and 50 for presentation to friends of Marguerite and Louis Henry Cohn. Bound in buff wrappers with hand-ties in envelope. Front cover printed in black: *THE FIRST WATCH*. Top and bottom edges trimmed, front edges untrimmed. Bradford Morrow (BM-199) notes a copy printed by the Grabhorn Press which is possibly in error. Not for sale. This pamphlet is easily one of Steinbeck's rarest publications, by virtue of the limitation alone, and is extremely difficult to find and if found, very expensive. The current price range is estimated at between $1,750 and $2,750. *References:* GP-A26a, BM-199 & 200, SRC.

13. *Foreword to* Between Pacific Tides (1948)

[Stanford, Calif.: Privately Printed], 1948. [viii]p.
(First and Only Separate Edition) This foreword is reprinted from the revised edition of *Between Pacific Tides*, by Edward F. Ricketts and Jack Calvin, Stanford University Press, 1948. Bound in blue

wrappers with thread ties. The front cover is printed in black: *John Steinbeck's/ FOREWORD/* to/ *"BETWEEN PACIFIC TIDES"/* 1948. Privately printed by Nathan Van Patten at the Stanford University Press. Van Patten was Director of the Stanford University Libraries at the time. There is some disagreement among Steinbeck specialists as to the exact number of copies printed. The estimates range from ten to twenty-five copies. Not for sale. This item is perhaps the rarest in this list of collectible Steinbeck materials. The current price range is estimated at between $3500 and $5000. *References:* GP-A28a, BM-205, SRC.

14. *The Forgotten Village* (1941)

a. New York: The Viking Press, 1941. 143p.
(First Edition) Contains 136 photographs from the film of the same name by Rosa Harvan Kline and Alexander Hackensmid. Published in May of 1941. Bound in coarse natural buckram. Drawing in green on front cover. Spine printed in green vertically from top to bottom: *STEINBECK•THE FORGOTTEN VILLAGE• VIKING*. Top edges stained green, all edges trimmed. Issued in a colored pictorial dust jacket printed in yellow, black and green. Originally priced at $2.50, with a current price range estimated at between $50 and $150. Copies of this edition are still relatively easy to obtain. *References:* GP-A14a, BM-135, NUC, CBI, SRC, BRL.

b. New York: The Viking Press, 1941. 143p.
(Book League Edition) This issue has: *BOOK/ LEAGUE* printed vertically on the spine of the dust jacket. Also on the verso of the title page [3] just below, *FIRST PUBLISHED IN MAY* 1941, is, *SECOND PRINTING BEFORE PUBLICATION*. Otherwise this issue is identical to the first edition. Originally priced at $2.50, with a current price range estimated at between $15 and $90. Copies of this edition are still relatively easy to locate. *References:* GP-A14b, BM-136, SRC, BRL.

c. Toronto: Macmillan, 1941. 143p.
(First Canadian Edition) Not seen. Published on the same day as the first Viking edition. Originally priced at $3, with a price range estimated at between $20 and $50. Copies of this edition are difficult to find. *References:* GP-A14c, CBI.

d. New York: [no publisher, 1941?] ?p.
(Program Preface) Not seen. This is a separate printing of Steinbeck's preface to the book. It appears in the program for the world premier of *The Forgotten Village* at the Belmont Theatre in New York City in November of 1941. Original price unknown. The current price range is estimated at between $50 and $200. Copies of this program are extremely difficult to locate. *References:* GP-A14d.

e. *Appeal from the Action of the Director of the Motion Picture Division in Refusing to License a Motion Picture Entitled The Forgotten Village. Petition for Review.* New York: Greenbaum, Wolff & Ernst, October 8, 1941. 56p.
(Unrecorded Legal Petition) Not seen. First and only printing of this legal petition to the Board of Regents of the State of New York by Pan American Films after the Motion Picture Division ordered that several cuts be made from the film before it could be shown to the public. This quarto document outlines the reasons *The Forgotten Village* was suppressed, stipulates which passages in the film were to have been eliminated, and outlines at considerable length why the film should be screened with its original contents. In their effort to demonstrate that Steinbeck's text and Kline's footage were not "indecent and inhuman" as the Motion Picture Division claimed, Pan American's attorneys quote testimony on behalf of the picture from numerous writers, critics, scholars—even Eleanor Roosevelt. Issued in wrappers. Not for sale. The current price range is estimated at between $500 and $900. Copies of this petition are extremely scarce. *Reference:* BM-137.

f. New York: The Sun Dial Press, [1944]. 143p.
(Sun Dial Reprint Edition) Not seen. Originally priced at $1, with a current price range estimated at between $15 and $25. Copies of this edition are difficult to locate. *References:* GP-A14e, CBI.

15. *El Gabilan 1919* (1919)

Salinas, Calif.: Salinas Index Pub. Co., [1919]. 79, [19]p.
Yearbook of the senior class of 1919 of Salinas Union High School. Contains contributions by John Steinbeck, associate editor and senior class president. There are advertisements on pages [81]–[96]. Bound in dark blue illustrated wrappers, printed in yellow and black. Original price unknown. The current price range is

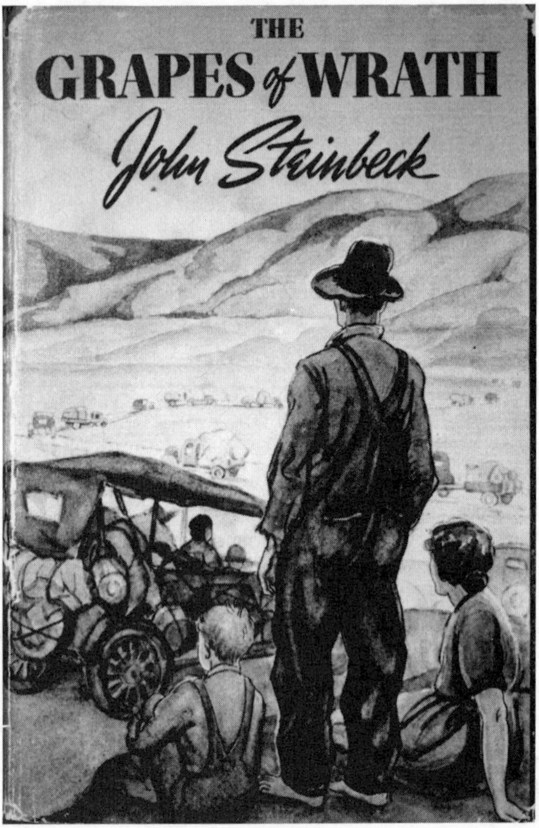

First edition of "The Grapes of Wrath" (with dust jacket).

estimated at between $1,000 and $2,500. Copies of this publication are extremely rare. *References:* SRC, BRL (photocopy).

16. *The Grapes of Wrath* (1939)

a. New York: The Viking Press, [1939]. 619p.
(First Edition) First published in April of 1939 in an edition of 50,000 copies. Bound in beige cloth with line drawings in reddish-brown on the lower half of the front cover. The lettering and decoration on the spine are also stamped in reddish-brown. A portion of "The Battle Hymn of the Republic" is printed in reddish-brown on the end papers. The top edges are stained yellow, all

edges trimmed. Issued in a colored pictorial dust jacket designed by Elmer Hader. On the lower right corner of the inner fold of the front dust jacket is printed diagonally: *FIRST/ EDITION*. Viking issued a salesman's dummy for *The Grapes of Wrath*. It contains the first nine pages of text with the remainder of the leaves being blank. This dummy copy is bound differently from the first published edition, in light gray cloth printed in blue on the spine and front cover. Also the title page varies entirely from the trade edition, with the title, author's name, and publisher printed in a different typeface. The Viking Press publisher's device (a viking ship) is present on the title page, as is the year of publication, both of which were deleted from the final title page design. The copyright page is blank in the dummy copy, where five lines of information are printed on the published page. The top edges are stained blue, instead of yellow. Noted in the Goldstone Collection is an offprint for bookseller containing pages 3–16 only (New York: The Viking Press, 1939). Originally priced at $2.75, with a current price range estimated at between $100 and $250. Copies of this edition are still relatively easy to obtain. *References:* GP-A12a, BM-103 to 105, NUC, CBI, SRC.

b. Toronto: Macmillan, [1939]. 619p.
(First Canadian Edition) Not seen. Published on the same day as the Viking Press first edition. The title page is revised to give the Macmillan imprint, and the dust jacket has the Viking imprints blacked out on the spine and flaps. Bound in beige cloth. Originally priced at $3, with a current price range estimated at between $200 and $400. Copies of this edition are difficult to find. *References:* GP-A12d, BM-109, NUC, CBI.

c. London: William Heinemann Ltd., [1939]. 553p.
(First British Edition) Not seen. Published in September of 1939. Bound in aqua blue cloth. The lettering on the spine is stamped in gold, and the Heinemann windmill is blind-stamped on the lower right-hand corner of the back cover. All edges unstained and trimmed. Has pink end papers. Issued in a rose dust jacket printed in reverse. Originally priced at 8s. 6d., with a current price range estimated at between $75 and $125. Copies of this edition are rather difficult to locate. *References:* GP-A12b, BM-108, EC.

d. New York: The Limited Editions Club, 1940. 2v. (559p.)
(Limited Editions Club Edition) Carries lithographs by Thomas Hart Benton in yellow and black and an introduction by Joseph

Henry Jackson. Published in a limited edition of 1,146 numbered copies signed by Benton. Bound in three-quarter tan grass cloth, with a brown rawhide spine. A pictorial shield is stamped in the center of the front and back covers. All edges are stained yellow and trimmed. Has pictorial end papers. There is a slip laid in each volume about the binding of the book. Both volumes issued in glassine dust jackets. They are contained in a publisher's tan paperboard case. The spine of this case had printed in brown: *STEINBECK [over shield]. THE/ GRAPES/ OF/ WRATH/ BENTON [over shield].* The Goldstone Collection contains an advance announcement with sample pages of the book. Originally priced at $15, with a current price range estimated at between $200 and $500. Copies of this edition are now very hard to find. *References:* GP-A12c, BM-111, NUC, CBI, SRC.

e. New York: Heritage Press, [1940]. 559p.
(Heritage Press Edition) Second illustrated edition, preceded by the Limited Editions Club two-volume set published earlier the same year. Illustrated by Thomas Hart Benton, with introductions by Joseph Henry Jackson and Thomas Craven. Some copies were issued in a deluxe leather binding while others were bound in coarse tan cloth. Has a publisher's paperboard case. Originally priced at $5, with a current price range estimated at between $75 and $225 depending on the binding. Copies of this edition are difficult to obtain. *References:* GP-A12e, BM-110, NUC, CBI, BRL.

f. New York: Literary Guild of America, 1940. ?p.
(Premium Edition) Not seen. Apparently a subscription publication. Original price unknown. The current price range is estimated at between $15 and $30. Copies of this edition are hard to find. *References:* GP-A12f, Bantam.

g. New York: Book League of America, 1940. ?p.
(Premium Edition) Not seen. Apparently a subscription publication. Original price unknown. The current price range is estimated at between $15 and $30. Copies of this edition are difficult to locate. *Reference:* GP-A12g.

h. New York: The Sun Dial Press, 1940. 619p.
(Deluxe Reprint Edition) Not seen. This deluxe edition apparently has a leather binding. Originally priced at $1.39, with a current price range estimated at between $15 and $50. Copies of this edition appear to be scarce. *References:* GP-A12h, CBI, Bantam.

i. New York: P.F. Collier & Son Corporation, [1940]. 619p.
(Collier Uniform Edition) Published in the uniform Collier binding of brown cloth with pictorial stamping in blue, maroon, and gold. Original price unknown. The current price range is estimated at between $20 and $40. Copies of this edition are difficult to locate. *References:* GP-A12i, BM-112, SRC.

j. Stockholm: Continental Book Company, [c1940]. ?p.
(Zephyr Books Edition, No. 28) Not seen. These English language editions were marked not for importation to Great Britain or the United States. Original price unknown. The current price range is estimated at between $50 and $125. Copies of this edition are very difficult to find. *Reference:* GP-A12j.

k. London: World Books Reprint Society, [1940]. ?p.
(A British Reprint Edition) Not seen. Dust jacket illustrated with portraits from the 20th Century Fox film version of the novel. Original price unknown. The current price range is estimated at between $150 and $300. Copies of this edition are very scarce. *References:* GP-A12k, MB-40.

l. New York: Garden City Publishing Co., [1940]. 619p.
(Special Reprint Edition) Not seen. This edition is bound in red leather with black and gold lettering and decoration on the spine. Apparently issued in a publisher's paperboard case. Original price unknown. The current price range is estimated at between $100 and $300. Copies of this edition are very difficult to locate. *References:* MB-39, NUC.

m. [Letchworth, Hertfordshire, Eng.]: Readers' Union, by arrangement with W. Heinemann, [1940]. 553p.
(Apparently a Reprint of the First British Edition) Not seen. Original price unknown. The current price range is estimated at between $20 and $50. Copies of this reprint edition appear to be very scarce. *Reference:* NUC.

n. New York: The Sun Dial Press, [1941]. 619p.
(Regular Trade Reprint Edition) There are three shades of binding noted for this edition and some copies omit the list of books by the same author from the verso of the half title. Also noted is a copy bound in light brown cloth stamped in dark brown which has a rare yellow wraparound band with comments by Dorothy Parker, Alexander Woollcott, and Clifton Fadiman. Originally priced at

$1, with a current price range estimated at between $100 and $275. Copies of this reprint edition are becoming difficult to locate. *References:* GP-A12l, BM-113, NUC, CBI, BRL.

o. Toronto: Blue Ribbon Books, [1941]. 619p.
(Canadian Reprint Edition) Not seen. Originally priced at $2.39, with a current price estimated at between $20 and $50. Copies of this edition are very difficult to locate. *Reference:* CBI.

p. New York: Doubleday Dollar Book Club, 1941. ?p.
(Doubleday Dollar Book Club Premium Edition) Not seen. Available to Book Club subscribers. Original price unknown. The current price range is estimated at between $15 and $30. Copies of this edition are difficult to locate. *Reference:* GP-A12m.

q. New York: The Modern Library, [1941]. 619p.
(The Modern Library of the World's Best Books, No. ML 148) This edition adds a "Note on the Author." Issued in a dust jacket with a Thomas Hart Benton drawing on the front cover. Originally priced at 95¢, with a current price range estimated at between $20 and $50. Copies of this edition are rather hard to find. *References:* GP-A12n, BM-114, CBI, SRC.

r. New York: Council on Books in Wartime, [circa 1943]. 480p.
(Armed Services Edition, C-90) Not seen. Published in paperback for distribution among military personnel during World War II. Not for sale. The current price range is estimated at between $50 and $100. Copies of this edition are very scarce and difficult to find. *Reference:* NUC.

s. New York: Council on Books in Wartime, [circa 1945]. 480p.
(Armed Services Edition, 690) Not for sale. The current price range is estimated at between $15 and $30. Copies of this edition, although scarce, are more plentiful than C-90. *References:* GP-12o, BM-115, NUC, SRC, BRL.

t. New York: Bantam Books, [1945]. 570p.
(First Bantam Paperback Edition, No. 7) Published in November of 1945 as indicated on the verso of the title page. Later Bantam editions list the publication date as January 1946. Bound in pictorial printed wrappers. Edges stained red. Originally priced at 25¢, with a current price range estimated at between $10 and $30.

Copies of this edition appear to be very difficult to locate. *References:* GP-A12p, BM-116, NUC, BRL.

u. Cleveland: World Publishing Company, [1947]. 468p.
(The Living Library Edition) Not seen. Includes illustrations by John Groth and an introduction by Carl Van Doren. Originally priced at $1, with a current price range estimated at between $15 and $30. Copies of this edition are becoming difficult to obtain. *References:* GP-12q, NUC, CBI.

v. New York: Mercury Publications, 1947. ?p.
(Condensed Edition) Not seen. This edition is an authorized condensation appearing on pages 77–123 of the series: *Bestsellers*, No. 7, published in the spring of 1947. Original price unknown. The current price range for this condensation is estimated at between $5 and $15. Copies of this edition appear to be very scarce. *Reference:* NUC.

w. [No place: No publisher, circa 1950] ?p.
(Pirated Edition) Not seen. Printed on cheap paper from an early Viking Press edition and bound in black cloth with title and author stamped in silver on the spine. This is a Taiwanese pirated edition. Original price unknown. The current price range is estimated at between $50 and $90. Copies of this edition are extremely scarce. *Reference:* BM-117.

x. Harmondsworth, Eng.: Penguin Books, [1951]. 416p.
(First Penguin Paperback Edition, No. 833) Published in July of 1951. Originally priced at 3s. 6d., with a current price range estimated at between $5 and $10. Copies of this edition are relatively difficult to find. *References:* GP-A12r, BNB, EC, WCBL, BRL, NUC.

y. New York: Harper & Brothers, [1951]. 619p.
(Harper's Modern Classics Edition) Not seen. Carries an introduction by Charles Poore. Originally priced at 95¢, with a current price range estimated at between $10 and $25. Copies of this edition are relatively scarce. *References:* GP-A12s, NUC, CBI.

z. New York: Bantam Books, [1954 and 1955]. 406p.
(New Bantam Paperback Editions) The *National Union Catalog* lists this Bantam edition (N2710) as being published in 1954. The Bibliographic Research Library has a copy of the same number

published in January of 1955. NUC also lists (F1301) which was probably published in September of 1955. Originally priced at 95¢ and later at 50¢, with a current price range estimated at between $2 and $4. Copies of these editions are fairly common. *References:* NUC, BRL.

aa. Garden City, N.Y.: International Collectors Library, [1958]. 473p. (Special Subscription Edition) This edition has a prospectus laid in. It was issued in two states of binding the priority of which is yet undetermined. While the bindings are similar they are easily distinguished by the end papers used. One issue has white end papers with an acorn and leaf design printed in blue, while the other has plain dark blue end papers. Issued in a dark blue imitation leather "William Morris" binding stamped in gold. The Bantam Books edition indicates that this edition was published in September of 1955 which is probably in error. Original price unknown. The current price range is estimated at between $40 and $90. *References:* GP-A12t, BM-118, NUC, BRL.

bb. New York: The Viking Press, [1958]. 619p.
(Compass Paperback Edition, No. C33) Originally priced at $1.95, with a current price range estimated at between $5 and $10. Copies of this edition are still relatively easy to obtain. *References:* GP-A12u, BM-120, NUC, CBI, BRL.

cc. New York: The Viking Press, [1958]. 619p.
(A Reissue of the 1939 Edition) Not seen. Originally priced at $5, with a current price range estimated at between $10 and $20. Copies of this edition are still relatively easy to obtain. *References:* GP-A12v, BIP.

dd. Louisville: American Printing House for the Blind, [1959]. 3v.
(Braille Edition) Not seen. Original price unknown. Price range and availability are not given. *Reference:* GP-A12w.

ee. New York: The Viking Press, [1962]. 619p.
(Book-of-the-Month Club Edition) Not seen. Original price unknown. The price range is estimated at between $5 and $15. Copies of this edition are still relatively easy to find. *References:* GP-A12x, BM-122.

ff. London: Heinemann Educational, [1965]. 424p.
(Modern Novel Series Edition). Not seen. Published on March 29, 1965. Commentary by Michaell Millgate. Originally priced at 12s. 6d., with a current price range estimated at between $15 and $30. Copies of this edition are relatively difficult to obtain. *References:* GP-A12y, EC, BBIP, WCBL.

gg. London: William Heinemann Ltd., [1966]. 416p.
(Heinemann Uniform Edition) Not seen. Published on June 20, 1966. Originally priced at 25s., with a current price range estimated at between $15 and $35. Copies of this edition are difficult to find. *References:* EC, BBIP, WCBL, (GP-A12aa?).

hh. New York: Franklin Watts, [1967]. 619p.
(Large Type Edition—"A Keith Jennison Book") Not seen. Originally priced at $9.95, with a current price range estimated at between $20 and $50. Copies of this edition are difficult to locate. *References:* GP-A12z, CBI, BIP.

ii. New York: Milestone Editions, [1967]. 510p.
(First Milestone Paperback Edition) This edition was set in Video Gael, a derivative of Caledonia, the very popular typeface designed by W.A. Dwiggins. Typography and design by Earl Tidwell. Original price unknown. The current price range is estimated at between $5 and $15. Copies of this edition are difficult to locate. *References:* MB-45, BRL.

jj. London: Twentieth Century Classics, [1969]. ?p.
(A British Reprint Edition?) Not seen. Original price unknown. The current price range is estimated at between $20 and $40. The availability of this edition is uncertain. *Reference:* GP-A12cc.

kk. [London]: Distributed by Heron Books, [1971]. 399p.
(Heron Uniform Edition) Contains illustrations by David W. Whitfield. Issued in a uniform imitation leather binding. Original price unknown. The current price range is estimated at between $100 and $200. Copies of this edition are very hard to locate. *References:* GP-A12dd, BM-124, NUC, CBI, SRC.

ll. New York: The Viking Press, [1972]. 881p.
(The Viking Critical Library Edition) Text and criticism edited by Peter Lisca. This edition adds critical apparatus and provides a number of Steinbeck's letters for the first time. Also has essays by

other critics and a bibliography. Originally priced at $8.95 hardbound, and in paperback at $2.95, with current price ranges estimated at between $10 and $20, and $5 and $10 respectively. Copies of this edition are common. *References:* GP-A12ee, BM-125 and 126, NUC, CBI, SRC, BRL.

mm. Chicago: J.G. Ferguson Publishing, [c1973]. ?p.
(U.S. Twentieth Century Classics Edition) Not seen. This edition appears to be reproduced from the same sheets as the 1969 British edition (see **jj**). Original price unknown. The current price range is estimated at between $5 and $10. Copies of this edition seem to be difficult to locate. *Reference:* BM-127.

nn. [London]: Pan Books, [1975]. 480p.
(Pan Books Paperback Edition) Published in August of 1975. Originally priced at £0.95, with a current price range estimated at between $5 and $7. Copies of this edition are relatively easy to find. *References:* BNB, EC, WCBL, CBI, BRL.

oo. Franklin Center, Pa.: Franklin Library, 1975. 589p.
(Franklin Library Limited Edition) Not seen. Contains illustrations by Robert Heindel. Original price unknown. The current price range is estimated at between $50 and $100. Copies of this limited edition, although scarce, are still available. *Reference:* NUC.

pp. [Harmondsworth, Eng., New York]: Penguin Books, [1976]. 502p.
(New Penguin Paperback Edition) Originally priced at $2.75, with a current price range estimated at between $5 and $10. Copies of this edition are quite common. *References:* BNB, CBI.

qq. London: William Heinemann Ltd., [1976]. 950.
(British Octopus Books Edition) Not seen. Combined edition with *The Moon Is Down, Cannery Row, East of Eden*, and *Of Mice and Men*. Originally priced at £3.95, with a current price range estimated at between $10 and $20. Copies of this edition are still quite common. *References:* BNB, CBI.

rr. Moscow: Progress Publishers, 1978. ?p.
(First Russian English Language Edition) Not seen. This edition has the text of the novel in English and a foreword in Russian. *Their Blood Is Strong* is included in the back of the book. Also in-

cludes some sixty pages of footnotes and pronunciation keys in Russian following the texts in English, for the use of Russian students. Original price unknown. The current price range is estimated at between $20 and $50. Copies of this edition are quite difficult to obtain. *Reference:* BM-130.

ss. Tarner, Margaret. *The Grapes of Wrath.* [by] John Steinbeck; retold by Margaret Tarner. London: Heinemann Educational, 1978. 131p.
(Heinemann Guided Readers: Upper Level Edition, No. 11) Not seen. Apparently a simplified version for young readers. Illustrated by Jenny Thorne. Originally priced at £0.70, in paperback, with a current price range estimated at between $5 and $10. Copies of this edition are quite common. *Reference:* BNB.

17. *How Edith McGillcuddy Met R L S* (1943)

Cleveland: The Rowfant Club, 1943. 18p.
(First and Only Separate Hardbound Edition) Published in a limited edition of 152 copies printed exclusively for members of the Rowfant Club by the Grabhorn Press of San Francisco in October of 1943. Printed on good quality wove *VIDALON-HAUT* paper. Bound in red decorative boards on a light gray background with the spine bound in black buckram. There is a red paper label pasted on the front cover stamped in gold: *[within a decorative border] How/ Edith McGillcuddy/ Met R.L.S.* Also there is a red paper label pasted on the spine, stamped in gold vertically from bottom to top: *How Edith McGillcuddy Met R.L.S.* The top edges are trimmed, and the front and bottom edges are untrimmed. Issued in a green dust jacket. Not for sale. The current price range is estimated at between $1,700 and $2,000. Copies of this limited edition are extremely rare and are almost never seen in booksellers' catalogs. *References:* GP-A20a, BM-169, NUC, SRC.

18. *In Dubious Battle* (1936)

a. New York: Covici-Friede Publishers, [1936]. 349p.
(First Edition, Limited Issue) Published in October of 1936 in a limited edition consisting of 99 numbered copies signed by the author. Bound in beige cloth on the covers and black cloth on the spine. The lettering on the spine is stamped in gold. The top edges

are stained red, and all of the edges are trimmed. Issued in a tissue dust jacket and a black publisher's case with an orange paper label printed in black: *IN/ DUBIOUS/ BATTLE/ [rule]/ STEINBECK*. There is noted an unrecorded printer's copy of this limited issue. Everything including the binding and the publisher's box is identical except, rather than being numbered this copy is out-of-series and designated as "Printer's Copy B." The location of a presumed "Printer's Copy A" is not known at this time, nor is it known how many lettered copies thus designated actually exist. Originally priced at $5, with a current price range estimated at between $1,900 and $3,000. The Printer's Copies are worth $5,000+. Copies of this limited issue are extremely rare and very expensive as are the Printer's Copies if such others exist. *References:* GP-A5a, BM-43 and 44, NUC, CBI, SRC.

b. New York: Covici-Friede Publishers, [1936]. 349p.
(First Edition, Regular Trade Issue) Also published in October of 1936. Bound in yellow cloth. There are red rules on the left hand and right corner of the front and back covers. The lettering and rules on the spine are stamped in red and black. The top edges are stained red, and all edges are trimmed. Issued in an orange and black pictorial dust jacket printed in black, orange and yellow. There is apparently a second printing of this trade edition. It is identical to the first printing except for the addition of: *SECOND/ PRINTING* to the spine of the dust jacket. Originally priced at $2.50, with a current price range estimated at between $300 and $500. Copies of this edition are very difficult to locate. *References:* GP-A5b, BM-45 and 46, NUC, CBI, SRC.

c. London: William Heinemann Ltd., [1936]. 304p.
(First British Edition) Not seen. Published in May of 1936. Bound in blue cloth. The lettering and rules on the spine are stamped in gold. The Heinemann windmill is blind-stamped on the lower right-hand corner of the back cover. All of the edges are unstained and trimmed. This edition has blue end papers. Issued in a colored pictorial dust jacket. Originally priced at 7s. 6d., with a current price range estimated at between $100 and $300. Copies of this edition are very hard to find. *References:* GP-A5c, NUC, CBI, EC.

d. Toronto: McLeod, [c1936]. 349p.
(First Canadian Edition) Not seen. Originally priced at $2.50, with a current price range estimated at between $75 and $125. Copies of this edition are very difficult to obtain. *References:* GP-A5d, CBI.

e. New York: Blue Ribbon Books, 1937. 349p.
(Apparently a Reprint Edition) Not seen. The *National Union Catalog* gives the date of this edition as 1936 which is probably just the original date of publication. Originally priced at 98¢, with a current price range estimated at between $75 and $150. Copies of this edition are difficult to find. *References:* GP-A5f (date given as 1939), BM-47 (date given as 1939), MB-18 (date given as 1939), NUC (date given as 1936), and CBI (date given as 1937). The 1937 date given by CBI seems the most likely to be correct. The others are probably later printings, except for the one given in NUC. *References:* GP-A5f, BM-47, MB-18, NUC, CBI.

f. Toronto: McClelland and Stewart Ltd., [1937]. 349p.
(Apparently a Canadian Reprint Edition) Not seen. Originally priced at $1.29, with a current price range estimated at between $35 and $75. Copies of this edition are difficult to locate. *Reference:* CBI.

g. New York: The Viking Press, [1938]. 349p.
(First Viking Press Edition) Not seen. The *National Union Catalog* lists a copy published in 1936, which is probably just the date of the first edition. The pagination is the same as the Modern Library Edition (See No. **h**, below). Originally priced at $2.50, with a current price range estimated at between $20 and $45. Copies of this edition are difficult to find. *References:* GP-A5e, NUC, CBI.

h. New York: The Modern Library, [1939]. 343p.
(Modern Library of the World's Best Books Edition, No. ML 115) Issued in a number of variant dust jackets. This edition, published in September of 1939, adds a biographical note on Steinbeck for the first time. Originally priced at 95¢, with a current price range estimated at between $25 and $45. Copies of this edition are difficult to locate. *References:* GP-A5g, BM-48, NUC, CBI, BRL.

i. New York: The Sun Dial Press, [1940]. 349p.
(Sun Dial Reprint Edition) Not seen. The dust jacket of this edition reproduces the same design of the first trade edition. Originally priced at 89¢, with a current price range estimated at between $15 and $30. Copies of this edition are difficult to obtain. *References:* GP-A5h, BM-49, NUC, CBI.

j. Shanghai: Modern Book Company, [c1940]. ?p.
(Apparently a Reprint Edition) Not seen. Original price unknown.

The current price range is estimated at between $50 and $100. Copies of this edition are extremely rare. *Reference:* GP-A5i.

k. New York: P.F. Collier & Son Corporation, [c1940]. 349p.
(Collier Uniform Edition) Published in the uniform Collier binding of brown cloth with pictorial stamping in blue, maroon, and gold. Original price unknown. The current price range is estimated at between $20 and $40. Copies of this edition are difficult to locate. *References:* GP-A5j, BM-50, NUC, BRL.

l. Cleveland: World Publishing Company, [1947]. 343p.
(Tower Books Edition, No. T-435) Published in January of 1947. Issued in a pictorial dust jacket designed by Leo Manso. Originally priced at 49¢, with a current price range estimated at between $15 and $25. Copies of this edition are still relatively easy to locate. *References:* GP-A5k, BM-51, NUC, CBI, BRL.

m. New York: Bantam Books, [1961]. 250p.
(First Bantam Paperback Edition, No. H2279) Published in October of 1961. Originally priced at 60¢, with a current price ranged estimated at between $5 and $15. Copies of this edition are relatively easy to find. *References:* GP-A5l, BM-52, NUC, BIP, BRL.

n. [London]: New English Library, [1962]. ?p.
(British Paperback Edition) Not seen. Original price unknown. The current price range is estimated at between $15 and $25. Copies of this edition appear to be scarce. *Reference:* GP-A5m.

o. New York: The Viking Press, [1963]. 313p.
(New Viking Edition) Issued without a dust jacket. Originally priced at $5, with a current price range estimated at between $10 and $25. Copies of this edition are relatively easy to locate. *References:* GP-A5n, BIP, SRC.

p. New York: The Viking Press, [1963]. 313p.
(Compass Books Paperback Edition, No. C132) Originally priced at $1.65, with a current price range estimated at between $3 and $7. Copies of this edition are still quite common. *References:* GP-A5o, BM-54, CBI, BRL.

q. London: Four Square Books, [1967]. 256p.
(New British Paperback Edition) Not seen. Published in June of 1967. Originally priced at 5s., with a current price range estimated at between $5 and $10. Copies of this edition are difficult to locate. *References:* BBIP, WCBL.

r. London: William Heinemann Ltd., [1970]. 279p.
(New Heinemann Edition) Not seen. Published in July of 1970. Originally priced at 35s., with a current price range estimated at between $10 and $25. Copies of this edition are relatively difficult to obtain in the United States. *References:* GP-A5p, BNB, BBIP, CBI.

s. [London]: Distributed by Heron Books, [1971]. 292p.
(Heron Uniform Edition) Bound in a uniform imitation leather binding with illustrations by Charles Bardet. Original price unknown. The current price range is estimated at between $100 and $200. Copies of this edition are very hard to locate. *References:* GP-A5q, NUC, CBI, SRC.

t. New York: Alexis Gregory and CRM Publishing (Del Mar, California), [1971]. 375p.
(First Nobel Prize Library Edition) Published under the sponsorship of the Nobel Foundation and the Swedish Academy. Combined with Faulkner and O'Neill. Also has the text of the Nobel speeches. Contains *In Dubious Battle* on pages 209–362 with illustrations by Fontanarosa. Original price unknown. The current price range is estimated at between $15 and $25. Copies of this book are still relatively easy to find. *References:* BM-55, NUC, SRC, BRL, GP-B175.

u. London: New English Library, 1973. 319p.
(A Later New English Library Paperback Edition) Not seen. Originally priced at £0.50, with a current price range estimated at between $5 and $10. Copies of this edition are somewhat difficult to obtain in the United States. (Later editions are noted). *Reference:* BNB.

v. London: Pan Books, 1978. 253p.
(Pan Books Paperback Edition) Not seen. Published in August of 1978. Originally priced at £0.80, with a current price range estimated at between $2 and $4. Copies of this edition are fairly common. *References:* BNB, CBI.

w. [Harmondsworth, Eng., New York]: Penguin Books, [1979]. 313p. (Penguin Books Paperback Edition) Originally priced at $2.50, with a current price range estimated at between $3 and $7. Copies of this edition are quite common. *References:* CBI, BIP, NUC, BRL.

19. *John Steinbeck: His Language* (1970)

Aptos, California: [Roxburghe & Zamorano Clubs], 1970. [14]p. (First and Only Edition) Published in a limited edition of 150 copies. Printed by the Grace Hoper Press. Contains text by James D. Hart, with a letter from John Steinbeck to Mrs. Katharine Carruth Grover as the frontispiece, and a translation of a poem from the Ukranian by Steinbeck printed in facsimile on p[5]. Issued in September of 1970 for a joint meeting of the Roxburghe and Zamorano Clubs. A folio bound in white wrappers. On the front cover in red is: *John Steinbeck/ HIS LANGUAGE.* There are no end papers. The frontispiece is tipped in p[2], and pages [5–6] are a cancel. Not for sale. The current price range is estimated at between $100 and $175. Copies of this pamphlet are very rare. *References:* GP-A45a, BM-279, SRC.

20. *John Steinbeck Replies* (1940)

a. [New York: Friends of Democracy, Inc., 1940] [4]p.
(First Edition) Mimeographed and published by Leon M. Birkhead, who was National Director of the Friends of Democracy. This leaflet prints a letter to Steinbeck from Birkhead asking him to respond to "widespread propaganda particularly among the extreme reactionary religionists of the country, that he [Steinbeck] is Jewish and that *The Grapes of Wrath* is Jewish propaganda." Steinbeck's reply is printed on the following page. Unbound and consists of a single leaf folded to make four pages. Not for sale. The current price range is estimated at between $100 to $200. Copies of this leaflet are extremely scarce. *References:* GP-A13a, BM-133, NUC, SRC, BRL (photocopy).

b. Stamford, Conn.: The Overbrook Press, 1940. [13]p.
(Second Edition, with New Title) Not seen. Has the following new title: *John Steinbeck, A Letter Written in Reply to a Request for a Statement about his Ancestry, Together with the Letter Origi-*

nally Submitted by the Friends of Democracy. Published in a limited edition of 350 copies printed by Arthur Altschul in September of 1940. Printed on good quality wove paper and bound in brown paper boards. There is a paper label on the front cover: A Letter by/ *[in red] John Steinbeck/ TO THE FRIENDS OF DEMOCRACY*. Issued in a clear cellophane dust jacket. Apparently not for sale. The current price range is estimated at between $200 and $450. Copies of this edition are very scarce. *References:* GP-A13b, BM-134, NUC.

21. *Journal of a Novel:* The *East of Eden* Letters (1969)

a. New York: The Viking Press, [1969]. 182p.
(First Edition, Limited Issue) Published in December of 1969 in a limited edition of 600 copies. Printed on good quality wove paper and bound in blue boards, with blue one-quarter cloth spine. The lettering on the spine is stamped in silver. All of the edges are unstained and trimmed. This issue has blue end papers. Issued in a glassine dust jacket and a publisher's case with a blue paper label on the front cover. Originally priced at $25, with a current price range estimated at between $75 and $150. Copies of this limited edition are still available but are rapidly becoming scarce. *References:* GP-A44a, BM-274, MB-102, SRC.

b. New York: The Viking Press, [1969]. 182p.
(First Edition, Regular Trade Issue) Published in December of 1969 in an edition of 1,000 copies. Bound in light blue cloth, with a navy blue spine. Lettering on the spine is stamped in silver. The top edges are stained blue, and all of the edges are trimmed. The end papers display a facsimile of the manuscripts. Issued in a decorative brown dust jacket designed by Virginia Smith. Originally priced at $6.50, with a current price range estimated at between $15 and $30. Copies of this edition are still relatively easy to locate. *References:* GP-A44b, BM-275, MB-103, NUC, CBI, SRC, BRL.

c. Toronto: Macmillan, [1969]. 182p.
(First Canadian Edition) Not seen. Published at the same time as the Viking Press regular trade edition. Original price unknown. The current price range is estimated at between $20 and $40. Copies of this edition are difficult to find. *Reference:* GP-A44d.

d. London: William Heinemann Ltd., [1970]. 182p.
(First British Edition) Not seen. Published in May of 1970. Bound in greenish-yellow cloth. The lettering on the spine is stamped in gold. All of the edges are unstained and trimmed. Issued in a white decorative dust jacket. Originally priced at £1.75, with a current price range estimated at between $25 and $40. Copies of this edition are somewhat difficult to obtain in the United States. *References:* GP-A44c, BM-276, MB-104, NUC, CBI, BNB.

e. New York: Bantam Books, [1970]. 242p.
(First Bantam Paperback Edition, No. R5659) Published in December of 1970. Originally priced at $1.45, with a current price range estimated at between $7 and $15. Copies of this edition are still relatively easy to locate. *References:* GP-A44e, BM-277, MB-105, BIP, SRC, BRL.

f. London: Pan Books, [1972]. 222p.
(First British Paperback Edition) Published in November of 1972. Originally priced at 40s., with a current price range estimated at between $5 and $10. Copies of this edition appear to be common. *References:* GP-A44f, BBIP, BRL.

g. New York: The Viking Press, [1972]. 182p.
(Compass Paperback Edition, No. C347) Has a cover portrait of Steinbeck by Emma Hesse. Originally priced at $1.85, with a current price range estimated at between $5 and $10. Copies of this edition are quite common. *References:* BM-278, CBI, BIP, BRL.

h. Tokyo: Hayakawa-shobo, 1976. 329p.
(Japanese Translated Edition) Translated into the Japanese by Isuzw Tanabe. Bound in red cloth with lettering stamped in black. All of the edges are trimmed. Issued in an illustrated dust jacket. Original price unknown. The current price range is estimated at between $10 and $20. Copies of this edition are difficult to find in the United States. *Reference:* SRC.

22. *The Leader of the People—Play* (1952)

McMahon, Luella, E. *The Leader of the People, A Play in One Act*. Dramatized by Luella E. McMahon from a story by John Steinbeck. Chicago: Dramatic Publishing Company, [1952]. 27p.

(First and Only Separate Edition) Based on the story from *The Red Pony*. Bound in yellow-orange wrappers. Current price is $1.50. No price range is possible since this play is still in print. *References:* GP-A9k, NUC, BRL.

23. *A Letter from John Steinbeck* (1964)

[Aptos, California]: Roxburghe & Zamorano Clubs, 1964. [12]p. (First and Only Separate Edition) Contains a letter by John Steinbeck on page [7] to Katharine Carruth Grover. Published in a limited edition of 150 copies, printed at the Grace Hoper Press by Sherwood and Katharine Grover. Bound in off-white wrappers. The front cover printed in red: *A/ LETTER FROM/ JOHN STEINBECK*. The top edges are trimmed, and the bottom edges untrimmed. Not for sale. The current price range is estimated at between $75 and $150. Copies of this publication are very scarce. *References:* GP-A42a, NUC, SRC, BRL (photocopy).

24. *A Letter from John Steinbeck Explaining Why He Could Not Write an Introduction for This Book* (1964)

a. [New York: Random House, 1964]. 7p.
(First Separate Edition) Not seen. This pamphlet is Steinbeck's tounge-in-cheek refusal to write an introduction for Ted Patrick's *The Thinking Dog's Man*, which Random House published (including the rather lengthy Steinbeck non-introduction) the same year. Bound in orange wrappers. Printing on the front cover is in black. All of the edges are unstained and trimmed. There are no end papers. Published on January 9, 1964. The number of copies is unknown. Not for sale. The current price range is estimated at between $300 and $500. Copies of this pamphlet are extremely scarce. *References:* GP-A41a, BM-270.

b. Patrick, Ted (Edwin H.). *The Thinking Dog's Man*. New York: Random House, [1964]. 150p.
(Inclusion as a Non-Introduction) Contains this letter or non-introduction on pages 3–10. The book was originally priced at $4.95, with a current price range estimated at between $25 and $40. Copies of this book appear to be scarce. *References:* GP-B145, SRC, CBI, NUC, BRL (photocopy).

25. *A Letter of Inspiration* (1980)

[West Covina, Calif.: Charles and Ingrid Sacks], 1980. [8 leaves, unpaged]
This pamphlet is a reprint of a letter written by John Steinbeck at the request of the editor of the *Monthly Record*, a magazine devoted to the inmates of the Connecticut State prison system. This letter appeared on page 3 of the June 1938 issue. Issued as a Christmas greeting (December 1980) and signed by the publishers. Published in a limited issue of 100 copies printed on brown Wausau text and in Press Roman Italic typeface. Bound in brown wrappers with thread inner ties. All edges trimmed and has a cover title. Not for sale. The current price range is estimated at between $10 and $20. Copies of this publication are now difficult to locate. *Reference:* BRL.

26. *Letters to Alicia* (1965)

[Garden City, N.Y.: Newsday, 1965]. [20] leaves.
Comprised of weekly newspaper columns in the form of letters addressed to Alicia Patterson Guggenheim distributed by Newsday Specials. Original price unknown. The current price range is estimated at between $40 and $100. Copies of this publication are extremely difficult to locate. *Reference:* NUC.

27. *Letters to Elizabeth: A Selection of Letters from John Steinbeck to Elizabeth Otis* (1978)

San Francisco: Book Club of California, 1978. 119p.
(First and Only Edition) This edition is limited to five hundred copies. Edited by Florian J. Shasky and Susan F. Riggs, with an introduction by Carlton A. Sheffield. Printed by the Plantin Press (Patrick Reagh), Los Angeles. Printed on Linweave Text paper with type set in Fournier types. Bound in three-quarter tan boards with the spine and one-quarter of the front and back covers bound in beige cloth. A paper label printed in black is pasted on the spine. There is a prospectus laid in. All of the edges are unstained and trimmed. Issued in a plain gray dust jacket with a reproduction on the spine of the label found on the cloth spine except that it is printed in earthy red. Originally priced at $40, with a current price

range estimated at between $100 and $150. Copies of this book are becoming scarce. *References:* BM-289, NUC, SRC.

28. *The Log from the Sea of Cortez* (1951)

a. New York: The Viking Press, 1951. 282p.
(First Separate Edition) This edition provides only the narrative half of the *Sea of Cortez* (1941), and adds Steinbeck's 67 page preface "About Ed Ricketts" for the first time. Published in September of 1951. Bound in maroon cloth. Lettering and decorations on the front cover and spine are stamped in gold. The top edges are stained red, and all edges are trimmed. Has a printed map in color of Lower California on both front and back end papers. Issued in a yellow, green, and white pictorial dust jacket designed by Robert Hallock. There is at least one variant binding noted. Bound in blue-gray cloth with the top edges stained blue. Originally priced at $4, with a current price range estimated at between $200 and $500. Copies of this edition are scarce. *References:* GP-A15c, BM-141, MB-50, NUC, CBI, SRC.

b. Toronto: Macmillan, [1951]. 282p.
(First Canadian Edition) Not seen. Published at the same time as the Viking Press edition. Original price unknown. Current price range is estimated at between $75 and $125. Copies of this edition are difficult to find. *Reference:* GP-A15f.

c. London: William Heinemann Ltd., [1958]. 282p.
(First British Edition) Published on September 8, 1958. Bound in blue cloth. Lettering and rules on the spine are stamped in gold. The Heinemann windmill is blind-stamped on the lower right-hand corner of the back cover. All of the edges are unstained and trimmed. Has a map, in color, of Lower California on both front and back end papers. Issued in a blue, black, and white dust jacket designed by Peter Curl. Originally priced at 18s., with a current price range estimated at between $100 and $225. Copies of this edition are very difficult to locate. *References:* GP-A15d, BM-142, BNB, EC, NUC, SRC.

d. London: Pan Books, [1960]. 320p.
(First Pan Books Paperback Edition) Not seen. Published on November 4, 1960. Originally priced at 3s. 6d., with a current price

range estimated at between $10 and $20. Copies of this edition are very difficult to find. *References:* GP-A15g, EC.

e. New York: The Viking Press, [1962]. 282p.
(Compass Books Paperback Edition, No. C120) Originally priced at $1.45, with a current price range estimated at between $5 and $10. Copies of this edition are common. *References:* GP-A15i, CBI, BIP, SRC, BRL.

f. New York: The Viking Press, [1962]. 282p.
(Reissue of the 1951 Edition) Not seen. Probably issued without a dust jacket. Originally priced at $4, with a current price range estimated at between $10 and $20. Copies of this edition seem to be fairly common. *References:* GP-A15h, BIP.

g. New York: Bantam Books, [1971]. ?p.
(First Bantam Books Paperback Edition, No. Q5798) Not seen. Originally priced at $1.25, with a current price range estimated at between $5 and $10. Copies of this edition are fairly common. *References:* GP-A15i, BIP.

h. [London]: Distributed by Heron Books, [1971]. 283p.
(Heron Uniform Edition) Includes photographs and illustrations. Issued in a uniform imitation leather binding. Original price unknown. The current price range is estimated at between $100 and $200. Copies of this edition are very hard to locate. *References:* GP-A15l, SRC.

i. Harmondsworth, Eng., New York: Penguin Books, 1976. 286p.
(First Penguin Books Paperback Edition) Originally priced at $2.50, with a current price range estimated at between $5 and $10. Copies of this edition are quite common. *References:* NUC, BNB, CBI, BRL.

29. *The Long Valley* (1938)

a. New York: The Viking Press, 1938. 303p.
(First Edition) Published in September of 1938. This collection of short stories includes "St. Katy the Virgin" which was published separately in 1936 as well as *The Red Pony*. All of the other stories were previously printed in magazines with the exception of "Flight" which appears here for the first time. Bound in terra-cotta cloth

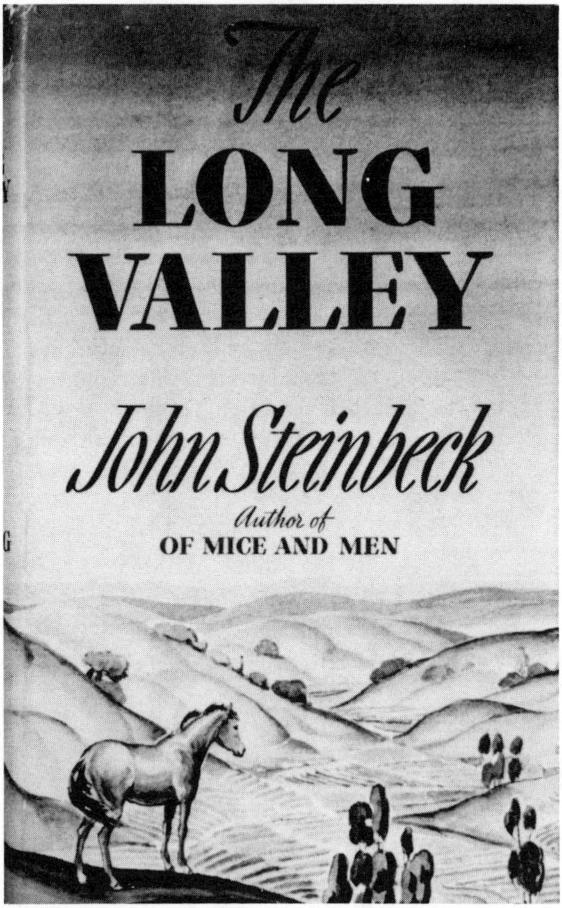

First edition of "The Long Valley," with dust jacket designed by Elmer Hader.

with a coarse beige buckram spine. Lettering on the spine is stamped in red. On the lower right corner of the back cover is the colophon, a Viking ship, printed in red. The top edges are stained in red; all of the edges are trimmed. Issued in a colored pictorial dust jacket designed by Elmer Hader depicting a horse standing on a hill overlooking a long valley. Originally priced at $2.50, with a current price range estimated at between $100 and $175. Copies of this edition are difficult to find. *References:* GP-A11a, BM-90, MB-31, CBI, NUC, SRC, BRL.

b. Toronto: McLeod, [1938]. 303p.
(First Canadian Edition) Not seen. Original price unknown. The current price range is estimated at between $75 and $125. Copies of this edition are very difficult to locate. *Reference:* CBI.

c. London: William Heinemann Ltd., [1939]. 314p.
(First British Edition) Not seen. Published in January of 1939. Bound in green cloth. Lettering on the spine is stamped in white. The Heinemann windmill is blind-stamped on the lower right-hand corner of the back cover. All of the edges are unstained and trimmed. Has buff end papers. No dust jacket has been noted. The contents of this edition are identical to the American except that "St. Katy the Virgin" in the American edition appears as "Saint Katy the Virgin" in the British edition. Originally priced at 7s. 6d., with a current price range estimated at between $50 and $100. Copies of this edition are difficult to locate. *References:* GP-A11b, CBI, EC.

d. New York: Garden City Publishing Company, 1940. 303p.
(De Luxe Reprint Edition) Not seen. Originally priced at $1.39, with a current price range estimated at between $20 and $40. Copies of this edition are difficult to obtain. *Reference:* CBI.

e. New York: The Sun Dial Press, [1941]. 303p.
(Sun Dial Reprint Edition) Not seen. Originally priced at $1, with a current price range estimated at between $10 and $25. Copies of this edition are scarce. *References:* CBI, NUC.

f. Toronto: Blue Ribbon Books, [1941]. 303p.
(Canadian Reprint Edition) Not seen. Originally priced at $1.39, with a current price range estimated at between $15 and $30. Copies of this edition are difficult to find. *Reference:* CBI.

g. New York: P.F. Collier & Son Corporation, [c1942]. 303p.
(Collier Uniform Edition) Published in the uniform Collier binding of brown cloth with pictorial stamping in blue, maroon, and gold. Stories from *The Long Valley* were published with the title of *The Red Pony* and with the title of *The Moon Is Down* including the title story. Original price unknown. The current price range is estimated at between $20 and $40. Copies of this edition are difficult to locate. *References:* GP-A11d, NUC, BM-94 and 95, SRC, BRL.

h. ... *13 Great Stories from The Long Valley*. New York: Avon Book Company, [1943]. 162p.
(Avon Modern Short Story Monthly Series, No. 9) This edition deletes "Johnny Bear" from the original collection. Originally priced at 25¢, with a current price range estimated at between $20 and $40. Copies of this edition are still relatively easy to obtain; however, ones in good to near mint condition are rare. *References:* GP-C52, BM-96, SRC, BRL.

i. New York: Council on Books in Wartime, [circa 1945]. 316p.
(Armed Services Edition, 794) Published in paperback for distribution to military personnel during World War II. Goldstone/Payne list this edition as being published in 1942 which is in error since none of the Steinbeck titles in this series were published before 1943. Not for sale. The current price range is estimated at between $15 and $30. Copies of this edition are difficult to find. *References:* GP-A11c, BM-93, MB-33, NUC, SRC, BRL.

j. New York: [Avon Book Company, 1945]. 230p.
(New Avon Library Edition, No., 77) This edition has the subtitle: "Fourteen Great Stories" and carries a cover painting in color by George A. Corrado. Originally priced at 25¢, with a current price range estimated at between $25 and $40. Copies of this edition are scarce. *References:* GP-A11e, BM-97, MB-35, NUC, SRC, BRL.

k. Cleveland: World Publishing Company, [1945]. 303p.
(Tower Books Edition, No. T-339) Published in February of 1945. Issued in a color pictorial dust jacket designed by Elmer Hader. Bound in terra-cotta cloth with the top edges stained green. Originally priced at 49¢, with a current price range estimated at between $15 and $30. Copies of this edition are still relatively easy to obtain but are diminishing in number. *References:* GP-A11f, NUC, CBI, SRC, BRL.

l. Stockholm/London: Continental Book Company AB, [1946]. 303p.
(Zephyr Books Edition, No. 41) Published as part of the "Library of British and American Authors" series for distribution on the continent only. Original price unknown. The current price range is estimated at between $25 and $45. Copies of this edition are difficult to locate. *References:* GP-A11g, BM-98, SRC (1948 printing).

m. *Fourteen Great Stories from The Long Valley*. New York: Avon Book Company, [1947]. 230p.
(New Avon Library, No. 132) This edition is exactly the same as No. 77 in this series except for the title and the design of the front cover. Issued in paper wrappers printed in yellow and blue. Originally priced at 25¢, with a current price range estimated at between $35 and $75. Copies of this edition are difficult to find. *References:* BM-99, NUC, SRC, BRL.

n. [New York?: Forum Books, 1948]. 303p.
(Apparently a Reprint Edition) Not seen. Originally priced at $1, with a current price range estimated at between $20 and $40. Copies of this edition are extremely scarce. *Reference:* CBI.

o. Leipzig: The Albatross, [1949]. 254p.
(The Albatross Modern Continental Library Edition, No. 509) Not seen. Goldstone/Payne give the place of publication as Rome rather than Leipzig, and list the publication date as appearing on the recto of the title page. Original price unknown. The current price range is estimated at between $120 and $190. Copies of this edition are very scarce. *References:* GP-A11h, BM-100, NUC.

p. Tokyo: Nan'un-do, [1954]. 2v.
(Nan'un-do's Contemporary Library Edition) Not seen. Edited with notes by Kotaro Ishibashi. Preface and notes in Japanese. Original price unknown. The current price range is estimated at between $50 and $100. Copies of this edition are difficult to obtain. *Reference:* NUC.

q. New York: The Viking Press, [1956]. 303p.
(Compass Books Paperback Edition. No. C1) Not seen. Originally priced at $1.25, with a current price range estimated at between $5 and $15. Copies of this edition appear to be scarce. *References:* GP-A11j, CBI, NUC, SRC.

r. Toronto: Macmillan, [1956]. 303p.
(Canadian Version of the American Edition) Not seen. Original price unknown. The current price range is estimated at between $5 and $15. Copies of this edition seem to be difficult to obtain. *Reference:* GP-A11k.

s. London: Transworld Publishers, [1958]. 254p.
(Corgi Books Paperback Edition, No. 577) Not seen. Published on September 2, 1958. Originally priced at 2s. 6d., with a current price range estimated at between $5 and $15. Copies of this edition appear to be scarce. *References:* GP-A11m, BNB, EC.

t. New York: The Viking Press, [1964]. 303p.
(A Reissue of the 1938 Edition) Not seen. Probably a reissue without a dust jacket. Published in November of 1964. Originally priced at $5, with a current price range estimated at between $10 and $20. Copies of this edition appear to be common. *References:* GP-A11n, BIP, BB, NUC.

u. New York: Bantam Books, [1967]. 214p.
(First Bantam Paperback Edition, No. S3538) Published in December of 1967. Originally priced at 75¢, with a current price range estimated at between $4 and $7. Copies of this edition are quite common. *References:* GP-A11o, BIP, BRL.

v. London: William Heinemann Ltd., [1970]. 215p.
(A Reissue of the 1939 Edition) Not seen. Published in July of 1970. Originally priced at £1.75, with a current price range estimated at between $5 and $15. Copies of this edition are somewhat difficult to locate in the United States. *References:* GP-A11p, BBIP, CBI.

w. [London]: Distributed by Heron Books, [1971]. 238p.
(Heron Uniform Edition) Issued in a uniform imitation leather binding. This edition contains illustrations by Graham Brownridge. Original price unknown. The current price range is estimated at between $100 and $200. Copies of this edition are very hard to find. *References:* GP-A11q, BM-101, NUC, SRC.

x. London: Heinemann Educational Books, [1978]. 122p.
(New Windmill Series Edition) Not seen. Published in July of 1978. Issued for use in British schools. Contains a selection of eight stories from *The Long Valley*. Published in pictorial boards without a dust jacket. Originally priced at £0.95, with a current price range estimated at between $10 and $25. Copies of this edition are somewhat difficult to find in the United States. *References:* BM-102, BBIP, CBI.

30. *Molly Morgan – Play* (1961)

Lawrence, Reginald. *John Steinbeck's Molly Morgan; A Play in Three Acts*. Dramatized by Reginald Lawrence. Chicago: Dramatic Publishing Company, [1961]. 104p.
(First and Only Separate Edition) This play is based upon a story from *The Pastures of Heaven*. Bound in wrappers with all edges trimmed. Three variant colors have been noted with regard to the wrappers: gray, olive, and yellow. A later issue has a slip pasted on the copyright page changing the performance fees. Originally priced at 85¢, with a current price range estimated at between $25 and $50. Copies of this edition are difficult to locate. *References:* GP-A2g, NUC, SRC.

31. *The Moon Is Down – Novel* (1942)

a. New York: The Viking Press, 1942. 188p.
(First Edition, Issue in Wrappers) Published in March of 1942 in a limited edition of seven hundred copies. Sewed and wrapped in the dust jacket. All of the edges are unstained and untrimmed. The colored illustration on this wrapper was designed by Frank Lieberman. Although it is not certain, it is assumed by most knowledgeable Steinbeck specialists that this issue in wrappers was probably sent out in advance of the publication date of March 6, 1942. There is a point of issue noted on page 112. On line 11, there is a period larger than other periods between the words "talk" and "this." There is a salesman's dummy located in the Humanities Research Center at the University of Texas, Austin. This issue was not for sale. The current price range is estimated at between $200 and $400. Copies of this edition are very scarce. *References:* GP-A16a, BM-145 and 146, SRC.

b. New York: The Viking Press, 1942. 188p.
(First Edition, Issue in Cloth) Also published on March 6, 1942 in an edition of 65,000 copies. Bound in blue cloth. The front cover is blind-stamped with the title and a castellated rule. Lettering and rules on the spine are stamped in silver. The top edges are stained blue, and all the edges are trimmed. Issued in a blue pictorial dust jacket designed by Frank Lieberman. There are at least three distinct variants of this issue that have been noted. The priority of these variants has not yet been determined.

(A) The spine has a third silver rule at the bottom. On the verso of the title page is added: *"PRINTED IN U.S.A. / BY THE HADDON CRAFTSMEN."* The large period between "talk" and "this" on line 11, page 112 has been removed. On page 188, line 10 there is an "S" at the end of the line. The top edges appear to be unstained. This issue has a smooth-textured dust jacket. It is presumed by some booksellers that this issue might be a Book-of-the-Month Club edition.

(B) The spine has only two silver rules at the bottom. The verso of the title page does not list the Haddon Craftsmen. On page 30, line 16, there is a period above and a little to the left of the word "official?" On page 103, line 7, the last "e" in the word "overpeppered" is broken. On page 112, line 11, there is a large period between the words "talk" and "this." The top edges appear to be stained light blue. It has also been noted that there are copies of this variant where the top edges are unstained. This variant has the rough-textured dust jacket.

(C) Goldstone/Payne (A16b) record that other copies have on the verso of the title page the notation: *"PRINTED AND BOUND IN THE U.S.A. BY KINGSPORT PRESS, INC., KINGSPORT, TENN."* Copies printed by the Haddon Craftsmen and the Kingsport Press have the large period on page 112 removed. Otherwise they are the same in all respects as GP-A16b. Copies printed by the Kingsport Press are bound in both blue and maroon cloth.

Note: William Young and Company, formerly of Wellesley Hills, Massachusetts in their Catalogue 623, Item 185, issued in 1979, claim that variant (A) is actually the first issue to be released for sale. They further claim that this first issue weighs twelve ounces and bears the imprint of the Haddon Craftsmen and the first issue identified by Goldstone/Payne (A16b) weighs thirteen ounces and *does not* [italics added] bear the Haddon imprint. Unfortunately this confusion will have to continue until further information comes to light. Originally priced at $2, with a current price range estimated at between $400 and $550. Copies of these variants appear to be available, but in diminishing numbers. *References:* GP-A16b, BM-148 through 150, CBI, NUC, SRC, BRL.

c. Toronto: Macmillan, 1942. 188p.
(First Canadian Edition) Not seen. Published at the same time as the Viking Press edition. Originally priced at $2.50, with a current price range estimated at between $20 and $50. Copies of this edition are very difficult to locate. *References:* GP-A16d, CBI.

d. London: William Heinemann Ltd., [1942]. 120p.
(First British Edition) Not seen. Published in June of 1942. Bound in terra-cotta cloth. Lettering on the spine is stamped in white. The Heinemann windmill is blind-stamped on the lower right-hand corner of the back cover. Has buff end papers. All of the edges are unstained and trimmed. Issued in an orange and white dust jacket. Also noted in a variant brown cloth binding. Originally priced at 5s., with a price range estimated at between $25 and $75. Copies of this edition are hard to find. *References:* GP-A16c, BM-151, CBI, NUC.

e. New York: The Viking Press, 1942. 188p.
(Book-of-the-Month Club Edition) Perhaps this is variant (A) in No. 2 on the previous page. Original price unknown. The current price range is estimated at between $20 and $50. Copies of this edition are relatively common. *References:* GP-A16e, BRL.

f. London [Melbourne, Australia]: Heinemann, [1942]. 128p.
(First Australian Edition) Not seen. London is given on the title page as the place of publication but the following is contained on the verso: "First Published 1942/ First Australian Edition/ October 1942..." Bound in light brown cloth with the lettering on the spine stamped in white. Issued in a coated paper dust jacket which reproduces a revised version of the Lieberman illustration used on the Viking Press edition. Original price unknown. The current price range is estimated at between $100 and $175. Copies of this edition are very scarce. *Reference:* BM-152.

g. Stockholm: Continental Book Company, 1942. 187p.
(First Clipper Books Edition) Not seen. Not for importation into Great Britain or the United States. Bound in light blue, three-quarter cloth with dark blue boards. Apparently published by the same company which produced the Zephyr Books Edition, No. 16 in 1945. Original price unknown. The current price range is estimated at between $100 and $175. Copies of this edition are very scarce. *References:* BM-153, NUC.

h. Garden City, N.Y.: The Sun Dial Press, 1943. 188p.
(Sun Dial Reprint Edition) Apparently this edition was reprinted from the plates of the first Viking Press edition. The large period on page 112, line 11, between the words "talk" and "this" is there. This edition is illustrated with photographs from the Twentieth Century–Fox production of the movie starring Lee J. Cobb and Sir

Cedric Hardwicke. There are variants bound in greenish-gray and blue cloth. The title page states "Published by Permission of the Viking Press, Inc." Some copies in blue cloth omit this statement on the title page. The dust jacket depicts a scene from the movie version. Originally priced at $1, with a current price range estimated at between $30 and $85. Copies of this edition are scarce. *References:* GP-A16f, BM-154, CBI, MB-53, NUC, SRC.

i. Toronto: McClelland and Stewart, 1943. 188p.
(Canadian Reprint Edition) Not seen. Originally priced at $1.39, with a current price range estimated at between $30 and $85. Copies of this edition are very difficult to locate. *Reference:* CBI.

j. Washington: Infantry Journal Penguin Books, [1943]. 119p.
(A Fighting Forces Penguin Special Paperback Edition, No. S219) Published in November of 1943, this wartime edition was issued for consumption by the American military with an extra page bound in at the back advising the reader to pass the book on to a friend in the armed services. Originally priced at 25¢, with a current price range estimated at between $40 and $95. Copies of this edition are very difficult to obtain. *References:* GP-A16g, BM-155, MB-54, SRC.

k. London: Heinemann, [1943]. 128p.
(Middle East Edition) Not seen. Original price unknown. The current price range is estimated at between $20 and $45. Copies of this edition are very scarce. *Reference:* GP-A16h.

l. London: Heinemann, [1943]. 89p.
(Armed Forces Edition) Not seen. Original price unknown. The current price range is estimated at between $50 and $125. Copies of this edition are extremely rare. *Reference:* NUC.

m. London: Pan Books, [1958]. 142p.
(Pan Books Paperback Edition, No. G188) Not seen. Published on July 18, 1958. Originally priced at 2s. 6d., with a current price range estimated at between $15 and $35. Copies of this edition are difficult to find. *References:* GP-A16i, BNB, EC, BBIP.

n. New York: Barnes & Noble, 1962. 610p.
(Combined Edition) Not seen. Combined with *A Tale of Two*

Cities by Charles Dickens. Originally priced at $2.77, with a current price range estimated at between $10 and $25. Copies of this edition are now difficult to locate. *References:* GP-A16j, CBI.

o. New York: P.F. Collier & Son Corporation, [c1962]. 188p. & 186p. (Collier Uniform Edition) Published in the uniform Collier binding of brown cloth with pictorial stamping in blue, maroon, and gold. Also includes ten of Steinbeck's short stories with the title *The Long Valley*. On the spine reads: *The Moon Is Down* and *Short Stories*. Each book has a separate title page. Original price unknown. The current price range is estimated at between $30 and $55. Copies of this edition are difficult to locate. *References:* GP-A16k, BM-156, NUC, BRL.

p. Toronto: Macmillan, [1963]. 122p.
(Canadian Edition with Study Guide) Not seen. Issued with study material prepared by Lawrence Darby. CBI lists this edition as being published in 1969. It is not known if the CBI listing is just a reprint or if Goldstone/Payne have made an error. CBI lists the original price as $1.50. The current price range is estimated at between $15 and $40. Copies of this edition appear to be scarce. *References:* GP-A161, CBI (1969).

q. New York: Bantam Books, [1964]. 115p.
(First Bantam Books Paperback Edition, No. F2711) Published in February of 1964. Originally priced at 50¢, with a current price range estimated at between $5 and $15. Copies of this edition are still fairly common. *References:* GP-A16m, BM-157, MB-55, BIP, NUC, BRL.

r. London: Heinemann Educational Books, [1966]. 123p.
(New Windmill Series Edition, No. 101) Not seen. Published on October 3, 1966. Issued for use in schools. Originally priced at 6s., with a current price range estimated at between $10 and $25. Copies of this edition are difficult to find. *References:* GP-A16n, BNB, EC, BBIP, NUC.

s. New York: Bantam Books, 1966. 115p.
(Bantam Pathfinder Paperback Edition, No. HP4328) Originally priced at 60¢, with a current price range estimated at between $2 and $4. Copies of this edition are quite common. *References:* NUC, BIP, BRL.

t. London: Heinemann, [1968]. 120p.
(Apparently a Reissue of the 1942 Edition) Not seen. Published in December of 1968. Originally priced at 21s., with a current price range estimated at between $15 and $35. Copies of this edition are difficult to locate. *References:* GP-A16o, BNB, BBIP.

u. New York: The Viking Press, [1970]. 188p.
(Compass Books Paperback Edition, No. C292) Published with a new cover design by Edgar Blakeney. Originally priced at $1.95, with a current price range estimated at between $5 and $10. Copies of this edition are still quite common. *References:* GP-A16p, BM-158, NUC, BRL.

v. New York: The Viking Press, [1970]. 188p.
(A Reissue of the 1942 Edition) Not seen. Original price unknown. The current price range is estimated at between $10 and $30. Copies of this edition are still relatively common. *References:* GP-A16q, NUC.

w. [London]: Distributed by Heron Books, [1971]. 227p.
(Heron Uniform Edition) Issued in a uniform imitation leather binding and combined with *Burning Bright*. Illustrated by Robert C. Bates. Original price unknown. The current price range is estimated at between $100 and $200. Copies of this edition are difficult to locate. *References:* GP-A16x, NUC, CBI, SRC.

x. Paine, Michael John. *The Moon Is Down*, [by] John Steinbeck; retold by M.J. Paine. London: Heinemann Educational Books, 1975. 71p.
(Heinemann Guided Readers Paperback Edition; intermediate, No. 13) Not seen. Published in April of 1975. Illustrated by Clifford Bagly. Originally priced at £0.38, with a current price range estimated at between $5 and $10. Copies of this edition are somewhat difficult to find in the United States. *References:* BNB, BBIP.

y. Harmondsworth, Eng., New York: Penguin Books, 1982. 188p.
(First Penguin Paperback Edition) Originally priced at $3.95. No price range indicated. Still in print and quite common. *References:* CBI, BRL.

32. *The Moon Is Down—Play* (1942)

a. [New York]: Dramatists Play Service, Inc., [1942]. 101p.
(First Edition, First Issue) This is the dramatic version of the novel. Illustrated with photographs of the April 1942 production of the play, produced by Oscar Serlin and directed by Chester Erskin. Bound in stiff yellow wrappers printed in black. Lettering on the spine is also printed in black. All of the edges are unstained and trimmed. There are no end papers, and all advertisements are printed on the verso of the front cover. In this first issue 1,250 sets of sheets were printed on thick paper and has a sheet bulk measuring 12mm. 250 of these sheets were turned over to The Viking Press. A second edition was published by the Dramatists Play Service identical to the first edition except it was printed on thinner paper with sheet bulk of 8mm. and measuring 186mm. in height. Originally priced at 75¢, with a current price range estimated at between $175 and $250. Copies of this edition are scarce. *References:* GP-A17o, BM-159, NUC, CBI, SRC.

b. New York: The Viking Press, 1942. 101p.
(First Edition, Second Issue) Bound in blue cloth. Rules and lettering on the front cover and spine are stamped in blue. All of the edges are unstained and trimmed. Issued in light buff pictorial dust jacket printed in blue. This edition is comprised of the 250 sets of sheets printed by the Dramatists Play Service. The title page is reprinted with the binding and dust jacket supplied by The Viking Press. Originally priced at $1.75, with a current price range estimated at between $75 and $125. Copies of this edition are very scarce. *References:* GP-A17b, BM-160, NUC, SRC.

c. New York: A.L. Williams, agent, [1942]. 1v. (various pagings)
(Typescript Carbon Copy Edition) Not seen. Not for sale. The current price range is estimated at between $500 and $1500. Very few copies of this rare typescript edition exist. *Reference:* NUC.

d. London: English Theatre Guild Ltd., [1943]. 96p.
(First British Edition; Guild Library) Not seen. Bound in stiff red wrappers printed in black on the front cover and the spine. All of the edges are unstained and trimmed. There are no end papers. Advertising matter is contained on pages 89–96. Originally priced at 4s., with a current price range estimated at between $25 and $75. Copies of this edition are extremely scarce. *References:* GP-A17c, RC, Brit. Mus.

33. *Nothing So Monstrous* (1936)

a. [New York: The Pynson Printers], 1936. 30, [2]p.
(First Separate Edition, with New Title) This is a separate printing of an episode from *The Pastures of Heaven*. Published in December of 1936. Elmer Adler promoted the publication of this episode for himself and four other subscribers to use as Christmas gifts. The limited supply of paper for the binding permitted only 370 copies to be printed. There were to be 50 copies for Elmer Adler, 100 for Frederick B. Adams, Jr., 150 for Ben Abramson, 50 for Edwin J. Beinecke, and 20 for Howard Mott. For some reason, unknown in 1974, no copies were printed for Mott and copies exist without a name on the presentation page. However, in 1978, according to Bradford Morrow, Howard Mott located a copy of the issue with his name printed in the colophon. Bound in marbled boards, with an orange buckram spine, printed in black: *[ornament] Nothing so monstrous [ornament]*. The front edges are untrimmed, and the other edges are trimmed. First issued in a tissue dust cover. Contains pen and ink drawings by Donald McKay. Printed on good quality wove paper. Not for sale. The current price range for this limited issue is estimated at between $600 and $1,100. Copies of this edition are very scarce. *References:* GP-A2f, BM-16, NUC, SRC.

b. Folcroft, Pa.: Folcroft Library Editions, 1977. 30, [2]p.
(Folcroft Reprint Edition) Not seen. Originally priced at $8.50. No price range is indicated as this reissue is still in print. *References:* NUC, CBI, BIP.

c. Norwood, Pa.: Norwood Editions, 1978. 30, [2]p.
(Norwood Reprint Edition) Not seen. Originally priced at $8.50. No price range is indicated as this reissue is still in print. *References:* NUC, CBI.

d. Belfast, Me.: Porter, 1979. 30, [2]p.
(Porter Reprint Edition) Not seen. Originally priced at $24.50. No price range is indicated as this reissue is still in print. *Reference:* CBI.

e. [Philadelphia]: Richard West, 1980. 30, [2]p.
(Richard West Reprint Edition) Originally priced at $10. No price range is indicated as this reissue is still in print. *Reference:* BRL.

34. *Of Mice and Men—Novel* (1937)

a. New York: Covici-Friede Publishers, [1937]. 186p.
(First Edition, First Issue) This issue was designed by Robert Josephy and first announced for publication on February 6, 1937, in an edition of 2,500 copies. Three hundred copies of this edition were sent out for review containing a review notice mounted on the free front end paper. Bound in beige cloth. Thick rules on front cover are stamped in black and lettering resulting from reverse printing of a terra-cotta panel. The same is reproduced on the spine only smaller, and the words Covici•Friede are printed in terra-cotta at the base of the spine. The top edges are stained light blue, and all of the edges are trimmed. Issued in a pictorial dust jacket printed in black. On page 9, lines 20 and 21 read: "...and only moved because the heavy hands were pendula." These nine words were removed in subsequent printings and the entire page reset. On page 88 there is a bullet (a small dot or period) between the eights of the page numbers, which was removed in subsequent printings. Later issues have the top edges unstained and are printed and bound by Haddon. The Goldstone Collection contains a salesman's dummy with text to page 16. Inscribed: "For the salesman John Steinbeck 37." Catalogue No. 623 of William Young and Company indicates the existence of two unique copies of this first issue. There is in their copy "On the verso of the title page, the designer of the book, Robert Josephy has written: 'One of two copies first off the press before staining.' And at the bottom of the page where he is listed as 'designer' he has noted 'ruined by Josephy.' The sheets are unstained. It is obvious that only two bibliographically complete Steinbeck collections can ever exist, that is, provided the second copy is ever found. It is interesting to see that our colleagues in this field blithely ignore the existence of this book and continue to catalogue their second-state copies incorrectly. Josephy gave this copy to Steinbeck, who presented it to his regular book designer, Robert Rau, with the inscription 'For Robert Rau—John Steinbeck.' " With regard to the above, Mr. James M. Dourgarian, a bookseller and experienced Steinbeck collector, has this to say: "...this one of two books is simply a printer's copy...and not really the first issue. As the catalogue listing seems to indicate, the Josephy notations were made by hand, not type, whether they were the first two off the press or not. From a bibliographic point of view...the only true difference between these supposedly two copies and what they claim to be the first edition, second issue (first edition, first issue according to Goldstone/

Payne) is that these two are not stained. That being the case, and taking into consideration that there were probably printers copies of each of Steinbeck's books (or anyone else's for that matter), I fail to see the big deal. Certainly the books mentioned by William Young and Company would be a wonderful item and certainly more valuable than a 'regular' first edition copy, but $3,500? I don't think so and I remain dubious about calling what has been the first edition, first issue a first edition, second issue. There is an implied feeling, as well via this listing that what they would call a first edition, second issue somehow is now less valuable that what has been the going rate." Originally priced at $2, with a current price range estimated at between $350 and $750. Copies of this edition are very scarce. *References:* GP-A7a, BM-58 and 59, NUC, CBI, MB-21, SRC.

b. New York: Covici-Friede Publishers, [1937]. 186p.
(First Edition, Second Issue) The title page and binding are the same as in the first edition, first issue. Published on February 26, 1937. Page 9 reset with the exclusion of the original nine words. The bullet has been removed from the page number on page 88. The dust jacket is also the same. Originally priced at $2, with a current price range estimated at between $150 and $350. Copies of this edition are scarce. *References:* GP-A7b, SRC, BRL.

c. London & Toronto: William Heinemann Ltd., [1937]. 164p.
(First British Edition) Not seen. Published in September of 1937, with decorations by Michael Rothstein. Bound in blue cloth. Lettering on the spine is stamped in gold. The Heinemann windmill is blind-stamped on the lower right-hand corner of the book cover. Top edges are stained blue and all edges are trimmed. Issued in a blue dust jacket printed in black, with a drawing by Rothstein. Several variants have been noted of this edition. One has the top edges stained pink with all edges being trimmed. This variant also has pink end papers and was issued in a white pictorial dust jacket printed in pink and black. Another variant copy is noted with the Rothstein blue pictorial dust jacket printed in black and pink with the top edges stained pink and the same color end papers. Originally priced at 6s., with a current price range estimated at between $150 and $375. Copies of this edition are very scarce. *References:* GP-A7c, BM-60, RC, EC, CBI.

d. New York: Covici-Friede Publishers, [1937]. 186p.
(Book-of-the-Month Club Edition) Not seen. Published in March of 1937. Original price unknown. The current price range is estimated at between $30 and $75. Copies of this edition appear to be scarce. *References:* GP-A73, Bantam.

e. Toronto: McLeod, [1937]. 186p.
(First Canadian Edition) Not seen. Originally priced at $2.25, with a current price range estimated at between $50 and $125. Copies of this edition are very difficult to locate. *References:* GP-A7f, CBI.

f. New York: Blue Ribbon Books, [1938]. 186p.
(Apparently a Reprint Edition) Not seen. Published in March of 1938. Originally priced at 39¢, with a current price range estimated at between $25 and $50. Copies of this edition are difficult to locate. *References:* GP-A7i, CBI, Bantam.

g. Toronto: McClelland & Stewart, 1938. 186p.
(Canadian Reprint Edition) Not seen. Originally priced at 49¢, with a current price range estimated at between $25 and $50. Copies of this edition are scarce. *Reference:* CBI.

h. New York: The Modern Library, [1938]. 186p.
(Modern Library of the World's Best Books Edition, No. 29) Not seen. Published in March of 1938. This edition adds a preface by Joseph Henry Jackson. Variant bindings of red, brown, and blue cloth have been noted. Originally priced at 95¢, with a current price range estimated at between $25 and $40. Copies of this edition are scarce. *References:* GP-A7i, BM-62, NUC, CBI.

i. New York: The Viking Press, [1938]. 186p.
(First Viking Press Edition) Not seen. Published in August of 1938. Original price unknown. The current price range is estimated at between $20 and $40. Copies of this edition appear to be scarce. *References:* GP-A7h, Bantam.

j. Toronto: Macmillan, 1938. 186p.
(Apparently a Canadian Reprint Edition) Not seen. Originally priced at $1.10, with a current price range estimated at between $20 and $40. Copies of this edition are difficult to locate. *Reference:* CBI.

k. Leipzig, Paris, Belgrade: Issued by The Albatross, [1938]. 189p. (The Albatross Modern Continental Library, v. 366) Not seen. Apparently this was a special edition of only twelve copies printed on handmade paper and bound in half-leather. Not for sale. The current price range is estimated at between $300 and $750. Copies of this edition are extremely rare. *References:* GP-A7k, NUC.

l. New York: Triangle Books, [1938]. 186p.
(Apparently a Reprint Edition) Not seen. The actual publication date of this reprint edition is uncertain. Publisher's information on the verso of the title page of the copy cataloged by the Library of Congress gives the first printing as January 1937. Goldstone/Payne (A7l) give the date as [1940], CBI gives the date as 1938, and Bradford Morrow (No. 63) calls it a *bibliographical horror* with a ninth printing being issued in December of 1939. Originally priced at 39¢, with a current price range estimated at between $10 and $35. Copies of this edition are difficult to find. *References:* GP-A7l, BM-63, NUC, CBI.

m. London: Readers' Union by arrangement with W. Heinemann, 1938. 164p.
(A Reprint of the 1937 Heinemann Edition) Not seen. Original price unknown. The current price range is estimated at between $15 and $40. Copies of this edition appear to be difficult to locate. *Reference:* NUC.

n. New York: The Sun Dial Press, Inc., [1939]. 186p.
(Sun Dial Press Reprint Edition) Not seen. Goldstone/Payne give the publication date as 1937. Possibly this is just the original publication date of the first edition as listed on the verso of the title page, or there were two separate printings. The correct publication date is simply uncertain. Originally priced at 89¢, with a current price range estimated at between $20 and $40. Copies of this edition are difficult to obtain. *References:* GP-A7g, CBI, NUC.

o. London: Chatto & H., [1940]. 253p.
(Evergreen Books Edition, No. 23) Not seen. Published in December of 1940 and combined with *The Red Pony*. Originally priced at 1s., with a current price range estimated at between $5 and $20. Copies of this edition are scarce. *References:* GP-A7m, EC.

p. New York: P.F. Collier & Son Corporation, [circa 1942]. 186p.
(Collier Uniform Edition) Published in the Collier uniform binding of brown cloth with pictorial stamping in blue, maroon, and gold. Original price unknown. The current price range is estimated at between $15 and $30. Copies of this edition are difficult to locate. *References:* GP-A7n, NUC, BRL.

q. New York: P.F. Collier & Son Corporation, [circa 1942]. 303p.
(Collier Uniform Edition) Published with the title: *Of Mice and Men and Short Stories*. Includes *Saint Katy the Virgin* and *The Red Pony*. Published in the same uniform binding described above. Original price unknown. The current price range is estimated at between $15 and $30. Copies of this edition are difficult to find. *References:* GP-A7o, NUC, BRL.

r. London: Reprint Society, [1947]. ?p.
(British Reprint Edition) Not seen. Published with the title: *Two in One*. Combined with *Cannery Row*. Original price unknown. The current price range is estimated at between $15 and $30. Copies of this edition are scarce. *Reference:* GP-A7p.

s. Cleveland: World Publishing Company, [1947]. 186p.
(Tower Books Edition, No. T-436) Published in March of 1947. Issued in a pictorial dust jacket designed by Leo Manso. Originally priced at 49¢, with a current price range estimated at between $15 and $30. Copies of this edition are still relatively obtainable. *References:* GP-A7q, NUC, CBI, BRL.

t. [Paris]: The Albatross, [1947]. 189p.?
(Albatross Regular Trade Edition) Not seen. This edition was printed in Verona, Italy and published in Paris in association with the Librairie Marcel Didier. Goldstone/Payne give both the incorrect date (1949) and place of publication (Rome). They were apparently misled by erroneous information in the publisher's file since they state that they had not seen a copy of the book, and cite "Albatross" as a reference. Issued in yellow wrappers, with a white dust jacket printed in yellow and black. Bradford Morrow does not mention the Leipzig special edition published by The Albatross in 1938. Original price unknown. The current price range is estimated at between $50 and $100. Copies of this edition are very scarce. *References:* GP-A7r, BM-64, SRC.

u. Stockholm: Continental Book Company AB, [1948]. 186p.
(Zephyr Books Edition, No. 83) Not seen. This is a continental English language edition, not for distribution in England or the United States. Printed by Albert Bonniers Boktryckeri in Stockholm. Issued in white wrappers printed in black and red along with a white dust jacket printed in black, red, and yellow. Original price unknown. The current price range is estimated at between $90 and $150. Copies of this edition are very scarce. *Reference:* BM-65.

v. [Harmondsworth, Eng.]: Penguin Books, [1949]. 249p.
(First Penguin Paperback Edition, No. 717) Not seen. Published in October of 1949 and combined with *Cannery Row.* Originally priced at 1s. 6d., with a current price range estimated at between $5 and $15. Copies of this edition are difficult to find. *References:* GP-A7s, EC, RC.

w. Tokyo: Nan'un-do, 1954. 142p.
(Nan'un-do's Contemporary Library Edition) Not seen. The preface and notes are in Japanese. Edited with notes by Takashi Sugiki. Original price unknown. The current price range is estimated at between $10 and $30. Copies of this edition are very difficult to find. *Reference:* NUC.

x. New York: Bantam Books, 1955. 118p.
(First Bantam Books Paperback Edition, No. A1329) Published in May of 1955 in colored illustrated wrappers by Joseph Hirsch. Originally priced at 25¢, with a current price range estimated at between $15 and $30. Copies of this edition are becoming harder to locate. *References:* GP-A7t, BM-66, NUC, BIP, SRC.

y. New York: Bantam Books, [1958]. 118p.
(Bantam Classics Paperback Edition, No. AC12) First published in December of 1958. This edition is made up from the same sheets as the Bantam Books (A1329) edition, with different preliminaries and wrapper design which incorporates the Joseph Hirsch illustration on the cover used for earlier editions, but is otherwise completely different in layout and text. Originally priced at 35¢, with a current price range estimated at between $25 and $45. Copies of this edition are becoming somewhat difficult to locate. *References:* BM-67, NUC, BIP, BRL.

z. New York: The Viking Press, [1963]. 119p.
(A Reissue of the 1937 Edition Completely Reset) Issued without a dust jacket. Originally priced at $5, with a current price range estimated at between $10 and $25. Copies of this edition appear to be fairly common. *References:* GP-A7u, CBI, NUC, BIP, SRC.

aa. New York: The Viking Press, [1963]. 119p.
(Compass Books Paperback Edition, No. C125) Not seen. Originally priced at $1.25, with a current price range estimated at between $5 and $10. Copies of this edition appear to be fairly common. *References:* GP-A7v, CBI, NUC, BIP.

bb. London: Heinemann Educational Books, [1965]. 113p.
(New Windmill Series Edition, No. 95) Not seen. Published on December 13, 1965. Originally priced at 6s. 6d., with a current price range estimated at between $5 and $15. Copies of this edition are somewhat difficult to locate in the United States. *References:* GP-A7w, BNB, EC, BBIP.

cc. London: Heinemann, [1966]. 164p.
(A Reissue of the 1937 Edition) Not seen. Published in September of 1966. Originally priced at 21s., with a price range estimated at between $10 and $20. Copies of this edition are difficult to locate. *References:* GP-A7x, BNB, BBIP, CBI.

dd. New York: The Viking Press, [1968]. 119p.
(Viking Large Type Edition) A folio size publication with the text set in 18-point type for the use of "visually handicapped" readers. This was the first book published by Viking in this series. Originally priced at $6.50, with a current price range estimated at between $50 and $90. Copies of this edition are scarce; however, later printings are still in print. *References:* GP-A7y, BM-68, NUC, CBI, SRC.

ee. New York: Limited Editions Club, 1970. 164p.
(Limited Editions Club Edition) Published in a limited edition of fifteen hundred copies. Designed and illustrated by Fletcher Martin. Contains an introduction by John T. Winterich. Printed on good quality wove paper. Bound in three-quarter blue denim, with a brown leather spine. The spine is stamped in blind horizontally from top to bottom: *[within a rule]* of *MICE* and *MEN*. All of the edges are trimmed. Has brown end papers. Issued in a glassine dust

jacket and a publisher's brown paper case with blue denim edging. Originally priced at $20, with a current price range estimated at between $95 and $125. Copies of this edition appear to be scarce. *References:* GP-A7d, BM-61, NUC, SRC.

ff. New York: Heritage Press, [1970]. 164p.
(Heritage Press Reprint Trade Edition) Not seen. This edition is identical to the Limited Editions Club issue published in the same year, but in what is essentially a trade format. Issue in a publisher's box. Original price unknown. The current price range is estimated at between $35 and $55. Copies of this edition seem to be relatively easy to obtain. *References:* BM-69, NUC.

gg. [London]: Distributed by Heron Books, [1971]. 208p.
(Heron Uniform Edition) There is a general introduction by Walter Allen and the illustrations are by Robert C. Bates. Issued in a uniform imitation leather binding. Original price unknown. The current price range is estimated at between $100 and $200. Copies of this edition are difficult to locate. *References:* GP-A7aa, NUC, CBI.

hh. London: Pan Books, 1974. 95p.
(Pan Books Paperback Edition) Not seen. Published in October of 1974. Originally priced at 30s., with a current price range estimated at between $5 and $10. Copies of this edition are relatively common. *References:* BBIP, BNB, NUC.

ii. Winks, Martin. *Of Mice and Men* [by] John Steinbeck; retold by Martin Winks. London: Heinemann Educational Books, 1975. 87p.
(Heinemann Guided Readers Edition; Upper Level) Not seen. Published in paperback form in June of 1975. Illustrated by Gay John Galsworthy. Originally priced at 40s., with a current price range estimated at between $5 and $10. Copies of this edition are fairly common. *References:* BNB, BBIP.

jj. Harmondsworth, Eng., New York: Penguin Books, 1978. 270p.
(A New Penguin Paperback Edition) Combined with *Cannery Row*. Originally priced at $1.95, with a current price range estimated at between $4 and $7. Copies of this edition are quite common. *References:* NUC, CBI, BRL.

35. *Of Mice and Men – Play* (1937)

a. New York: Covici-Friede Publishers, [1937]. 172p.
(First Edition) Published on November 23, 1937. Bound in beige cloth. Lettering and ornaments on the front cover and spine are stamped in black and red. The top edges are trimmed and stained blue, and the front and bottom edges are trimmed. Issued in a blue and beige dust jacket printed in white. This edition of the play was designed by Robert Josephy. There are at least two copies of salesmen's dummies noted with the text printed up to page 16. One is in the Goldstone Collection and the other in the Valentine Collection. The latter copy like the former is handstamped "Nov. 5, 1937" on the front end sheet but does not bear the alteration in ink of the publication date from "5" to "23" as is in the Goldstone Collection copy. These salesmen's dummy copies were issued in a dust jacket. Originally priced at $2, with a current price range estimated at between $350 and $600. Copies of this edition are very scarce. *References:* GP-A8a, BM-72 & 73, NUC, CBI, SRC.

b. New York: Dramatists Play Service, Inc., [c1937]. 71p.
(First Acting Edition) Published in paperback with production notes. Originally priced at 85¢, with a current price range estimated at between $10 and $20. Copies of this edition are quite scarce. *References:* GP-A8b, BM-75, SRC.

c. New York: The Viking Press, [1937]. 172p.
(First Viking Press Edition) Not seen. Originally priced at $2, with a current price range estimated at between $200 and $500. Copies of this edition are very scarce. *References:* NUC, CBI.

d. Toronto: McLeod, [1937]. 172p.
(First Canadian Edition) Not seen. Originally priced at $2.25, with a current price range estimated at between $50 and $125. Copies of this edition are scarce. *Reference:* CBI.

e. [New York]: Dramatists Play Service, Inc., [1964]. 71p.
(A Reissue of the 1937 Acting Edition) Issued in wrappers. Original price unknown. The current price range is estimated at between $4 and $7. Copies of this edition are still relatively common. *References:* GP-A8d, BM-76, SRC, BRL.

f. Floyd, Carlisle. *Of Mice and Men; A Musical Drama in Three Acts.* After the novel and play by John Steinbeck. [New York]:

Belwin-Mills Publishing Corporation, [1971]. 206p.
(Piano-vocal Score, English) Folio, issued in wrappers. Covers designed by Evon Streetman showing a crushed mouse in Lennie's outstretched hand. This musical dramatic version of the play was commissioned by the Ford Foundation. Originally priced at $12.50. No price range is indicated as this edition is still in print and readily available. *References:* GP-A8e, BM-77, NUC, SRC, BRL.

g. Floyd, Carlisle. *Of Mice and Men; A Musical Drama in Three Acts*. After the novel and play by John Steinbeck. [New York]: Belwin-Mills Publishing Corporation, [1971]. 35p.
(Libretto, English) Published in wrappers identical to the piano-vocal score listed above. Originally priced at $5. No price range is indicated as this edition is still in print and readily available. *References:* GP-A8f, NUC, SRC, BRL.

36. *Once There Was a War* (1958)

a. New York: The Viking Press, 1958. 233p.
(First Edition) Published in September of 1958. First appeared in *New York Herald Tribune*, June 21, 1943, to December 15, 1943, as a series of dispatches from the European Theater of War during World War II. Bound in brown marbled boards, one-half yellow cloth. Lettering on the spine is stamped in red. The top edges are stained red, and all edges are trimmed. Issued in a colored pictorial dust jacket designed by Don Freeman. There is a variant binding noted in the Valentine Collection. This copy is bound in half yellowish-tan cloth, stamped on the spine in red, with brown boards. An extra strip of darker mustard-yellow cloth was bound across the top two inches of the spine, extending to both the front and back edges, where the cloth meets the boards. The words "John Steinbeck/ Once" are stamped in red on this strip, evidently to conceal a typographical error on the spine. It is possible that a number of copies exist with an error on the spine before this binding measure was taken by the publishers. Originally priced at $3.95, with a current price range estimated at between $85 and $375. Copies of this edition now appear to be difficult to find. The variant binding described above is extremely scarce. *References:* GP-A37a, BM-246 through 248, NUC, CBI, SRC.

OF
MICE
AND
MEN
A Novel by
JOHN STEINBECK
AUTHOR OF 'TORTILLA FLAT'

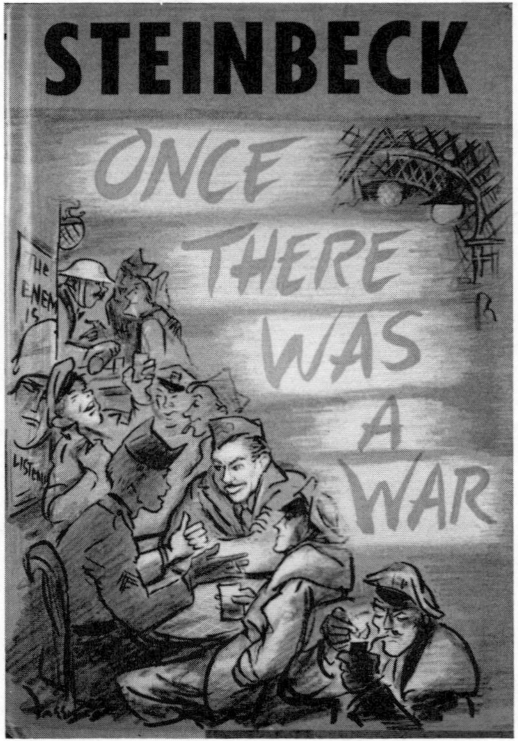
STEINBECK
ONCE THERE WAS A WAR

b. Toronto: Macmillan, 1958. 233p.
(First Canadian Edition) Not seen. Published at the same time as the Viking Press edition. Originally priced at $4.50, with a current price range estimated at between $50 and $90. Copies of this edition appear to be difficult to locate. *References:* GP-A37c, CBI.

c. London: William Heinemann Ltd., [1959]. 233p.
(First British Edition) Not seen. Published in December 7, 1959. Bound in black cloth. Lettering on the spine is stamped in silver. All of the edges are unstained and trimmed. Issued in a blue and black pictorial dust jacket which prints part of the text which is the description of Bob Hope entertaining GIs in a hospital on the back cover. Originally priced at 16s., with a current price range estimated at between $30 and $75. Copies of this edition are difficult to find. *References:* GP-A37b, BM-249, NUC, CBI.

d. [New York]: Books Abridged, 1959. ?p.
(Abridged Edition) Not seen. Published in March of 1959. Original price unknown. The current price range is estimated at between $10 and $30. Copies of this edition are very difficult to obtain. *References:* GP-A37d, Bantam.

e. New York: Bantam Books, [1960]. 173p.
(First Bantam Books Paperback Edition, No. A2079) Published in January of 1960. Originally priced at 35¢, with a current price range estimated at between $5 and $25. Copies of this edition are still fairly common. *References:* GP-A37e, NUC, BIP, SRC, BRL.

f. London: Transworld Publishers, 1961. 222p.
(Corgi Books Edition, No. 966) Not seen. Published in March of 1961. Originally priced at 3s. 6d., with a current price range estimated at between $5 and $20. Copies of this edition are difficult to obtain. *Reference:* BNB.

g. [London]: Corgi Books, [1967]. 141p.
(New Corgi Books Edition) Not seen. Originally published at 3s. 6d., with a current price range estimated at between $5 and $10. Copies of this edition are now difficult to find. *Reference:* BBIP.

Opposite: (Left) First edition of "Of Mice and Men" (in dust jacket). (Right) First edition of "Once There Was a War," with dust jacket designed by Don Freeman.

h. London: Pan Books, [1975]. 188p.
(First Pan Books Paperback Edition) Not seen. Published in November of 1975. Originally priced at 50s., with a price range estimated at between $5 and $10. Copies of this edition are fairly common. *References:* BNB, CBI, BBIP.

i. Harmondsworth, Eng.; New York: Penguin Books, 1977. 173p.
(First Penguin Books Paperback Edition) Originally priced at 70s. and $1.95, with a current price range estimated at between $5 and $10. Copies of this edition are quite common. *References:* NUC, CBI, BNB, BRL.

37. *The Pastures of Heaven* (1932)

a. New York: Brewer, Warren & Putnam, 1932. 294p.
(First Edition, First Issue) Published in October of 1932. Brewer, Warren & Putnam printed 2,500 sets of sheets, of which 1,650 copies were bound and approximately 650 copies sold. The remainder were sold to Robert O. Ballou in 1932. Bound in green cloth. Lettering on the front cover and spine is stamped in gold. The top edges are stained black and trimmed with the front and bottom edges rough trimmed. Issued in a silver dust jacket printed in blue with gold stars. Originally priced at $2, with a current price range estimated at between $600 and $1,250. Copies of this issue of the first edition are extremely rare. *References:* GP-A2a, BM-14, NUC, CBI, SRC.

b. New York: Brewer, Warren & Putnam, 1932. 294p.
(First Edition, Second Issue) Not seen. The exact date of publication is unknown. Also the exact number of copies published is unknown. This issue consisted of approximately 1,000 sheets, published in two states of binding and title page, by Robert Ballou, from approximately 1,850 sheets purchased from Brewer, Warren & Putnam. Bound in green cloth. Lettering on the front cover and spine is stamped in gold. The publisher's name, i.e. Robert Ballou is stamped in gold at the base of the spine. The top edges are stained black and trimmed, the front edges are untrimmed, and the bottom edges are trimmed. Issued in a silver dust jacket printed in blue with gold stars. The spine is stamped: *BREWER/ WARREN/ PUTNAM.* Two states of binding and title page have been noted but not described. Originally priced at $2.50, with a current price range

estimated at between $500 and $1,000. Copies of this issue of the first edition are very scarce. *References:* GP-A2b, BM-15.

c. New York: Robert O. Ballou, 1932. 294p.
(First Edition, Third Issue) The exact publication date of this issue is uncertain but possibly it occurred between October and December of 1932. Also the exact number of copies published is not known but the ones that were produced came from a portion of the 1,850 sheets sold to Robert O. Ballou by Brewer, Warren & Putnam earlier in 1932. A new title page was tipped in and the binding differs. These have not been descriptively recorded. Originally priced at $2.50, with a current price range estimated at between $400 and $900. Copies of this issue of the first edition are difficult to find. *References:* GP-A2c, SRC.

d. London: Philip Allan, [1933]. 302p.
(First British Edition) Not seen. Published in May of 1933. Bound in green cloth. Lettering on the spine is printed in black. All of the edges are unstained and untrimmed. Originally priced at 7s. 6d., with a current price range estimated at between $400 and $1,200. Copies of this edition are extremely scarce. *References:* GP-A2d, EC, NUC, CBI.

e. London: Quality Press, [1933]. 222p.
(First Quality Press Edition) Not seen. Original price unknown. The current price range is estimated at between $40 and $90. Copies of this edition are difficult to locate. *Reference:* NUC.

f. London: Philip Allan, [1934]. 302p.
(A Reissue of the 1933 Edition) Not seen. Published in May of 1934 in a cheaper edition. Originally priced at 2s. 6d., with a current price range estimated at between $50 and $90. Copies of this edition are very difficult to obtain. *References:* GP-A2h, CBI, EC.

g. New York: Covici-Friede Publishers, [1935]. 294p.
(First Edition, Fourth Issue) Not seen. This issue is comprised of the remaining portion of the approximately 1,850 sheets sold by Brewer, Warren & Putnam to Robert O. Ballou and by the latter to Covici-Friede. This final transaction did not take place until 1935. A new title page was tipped in, and the binding and dust jacket differ from the three previous issues. Bound in tan cloth. The front cover is printed in red with a horizontal rule extending across the spine and back cover. The spine is printed in red: *[orna-*

ment]/ THE/ PASTURES/ OF HEAVEN/ [rule] STEINBECK/ [ornament]/ COVICI/ FRIEDE. The top edges are stained light green and trimmed while the bottom edges are rough trimmed. Issued in a beige dust jacket printed in red. Originally priced at $2.50, with a current price range estimated at between $400 and $900. Copies of this edition are scarce. *References:* GP-A2e, NUC.

h. New York: Modern Age Books, Inc., [1938]. 154p.
(A Seal Book Unabridged Edition, No. 43) Published in paperback with typography by Robert Josephy. Bound in wrappers printed in black and red. All of the edges are unstained and trimmed. Originally priced at 25¢, with a current price range estimated at between $20 and $40. Copies of this edition are difficult to locate. *References:* GP-A2i, NUC, CBI, BRL.

i. Toronto: McLeod, [1938]. 154p.
(Apparently a Canadian Paperback Reprint Edition) Not seen. Originally priced at 45¢, with a current price range estimated at between $15 and $35. Copies of this edition are very scarce. *Reference:* CBI.

j. New York: Penguin Books, Inc., [1942]. 189p.
(Penguin Books Paperback Edition, Nos. 414 and 509) Not seen. Apparently No. 414 was published in August of 1942, and No. 509 was published sometime later that year. Original price unknown. The current price range is estimated at between $10 and $20. Copies of this edition are difficult to locate. *References:* GP-A2j, NUC.

k. New York: Council on Books in Wartime, [circa 1945]. 255[1]p.
(Armed Services Edition, No. 703) Published in paperback for consumption by the American military during World War II. Not for sale. The current price range is estimated at between $15 and $35. Copies of this edition are difficult to find. *References:* GP-A2k, NUC, BRL.

l. Cleveland: World Publishing Company, [1946]. 192p.
(Tower Books Edition, No. T-254) Published in February of 1946. Bound in dark green cloth. There are light green panels and decorations on both the front cover and spine. Lettering on the front cover and spine are the result of reverse printing and some are printed in light green. The top edges are unstained with the top and bottom edges trimmed and the fore edges rough trimmed. Issued in a colored pictorial dust jacket. Originally priced at 49¢, with a

current price range estimated at between $15 and $30. Copies of this edition seem to be available in limited quantities. *References:* GP-A2l, BM-19, MB-5, CBI, NUC, BRL.

m. London: Quality Press, [1946]. 222p.
(Possibly a Reprint of the 1933 Edition) Not seen. Published in October of 1946. Later editions have been noted. Originally priced at 7s. 6d., with a current price range estimated at between $15 and $30. Copies of this edition are scarce. *References:* GP-A2m, EC.

n. New York: Bantam Books, [1951]. 182p.
(First Bantam Paperback Edition, No. 899) First printing in May of 1951 and published in June of 1951. Published in colored pictorial wrappers. Originally priced at 25¢, with a current price range estimated at between $7 and $20. Copies of this edition are now somewhat difficult to find. *References:* GP-A2n, NUC, SRC, BRL.

o. London: Transworld Publishers, [1951]. 182p.
(Corgi Books Series Paperback Edition, No. 899) Not seen. Published in September of 1951. The *English Catalogue* gives the publication date as December of 1951 and Goldstone/Payne give the series number as SN1411. These differences are possibly the result of later printings. Originally priced at 2s., with a current price range estimated at between $5 and $15. Copies of this edition are difficult to find. *References:* GP-A2o, BNB, EC.

p. London: Ernest Benn Limited, [1953]. 222p.
(A British Reprint Edition) Not seen. A number of later reissues have been noted. Originally priced at 8s. 6d., with a current price range estimated at between $15 and $30. Copies of this edition are difficult to locate. *References:* NUC, EC.

q. Tokyo: Kinserdo, 1956. ?p.
(Modern English Series Edition) Not seen. Original price unknown. The current price range is estimated at between $20 and $40. Copies of this edition are scarce. *Reference:* GP-A2p.

r. New York: Bantam Books, [1956]. 183p.
(New Bantam Paperback Edition, No. A1478) Published in June of 1956. Originally priced at 35¢, with a current price range

estimated at between $5 and $15. Copies of this edition are somewhat difficult to find. *References:* BIP, NUC, BRL.

s. New York: The Viking Press, [1963]. 243p.
(New Edition Completely Reset) Issued without a dust jacket. Originally priced at $4.50, with a current price range estimated at between $15 and $30. Copies of this edition are somewhat difficult to locate. *References:* GP-A2r, BIP, NUC, SRC.

t. New York: The Viking Press, [1963]. 243p.
(Compass Books Paperback Edition, No. C133) Originally priced at $1.45, with a current price range estimated at between $7 and $20. Copies of this edition are relatively common. *References:* GP-A2s, BM-20, BIP, CBI, SRC.

u. Glenfield, Eng. [etc.]: F.A. Thorpe, [1969]. 233p.
(The Ulverscroft Large Print Series Edition, Fiction) Not seen. A number of later printings are noted. BBIP lists this edition as being published in December of 1968. Originally priced at 21s., with a current price range estimated at between $20 and $40. Copies of this edition are difficult to obtain. Later printings are still in print. *References:* GP-A2t, BNB, BBIP, NUC.

v. Harmondsworth, Eng., New York: Penguin Books, [1982]. 243p.
(New Penguin Books Paperback Edition) This edition carries a new cover design by Neil Stuart. Originally priced at $3.95. No price range is given as this edition is still in print and readily available. *References:* CBI, BRL.

38. *The Pearl—Novel* (1947)

a. New York: The Viking Press, 1947. 122p.
(First Edition) This novel first appeared in *The Woman's Home Companion* under the title "The Pearl of the World," in December of 1945. The first book edition was published in November of 1947. Illustrations and drawings are by José Clemente Orozco. Bound in brown cloth. The front cover has a drawing in black in the lower left-hand corner. Lettering on the spine is stamped in gold on a black background. The top edges are stained green, and all of the edges are trimmed. Issued in a red and blue dust jacket printed in white designed by Robert Hallock. There are two states of the first edition dust jacket. The first state has a photograph of Steinbeck

by Breitenbach on the back cover looking to his left. The second state has a photograph by the same photographer showing Steinbeck looking to his right. Originally priced at $2, with a current price range estimated at between $125 and $225. Copies of this edition are still relatively available. *References:* GP-A25a, BM-188 through 190, MB-71, NUC, CBI, SRC, BRL.

b. Toronto: Macmillan, 1947. 122p.
(First Canadian Edition) Not seen. Published at the same time as the Viking Press edition. Originally priced at $2.25, with a current price range estimated at between $50 and $125. Copies of this edition are difficult to find. *References:* GP-A25c, CBI.

c. London: William Heinemann Ltd., [1948]. 97p.
(First British Edition) Not seen. Published in October of 1948. Bound in blue cloth. Lettering and ornaments on the front cover and spine are stamped in gold on a black background. The Heinemann windmill is blind-stamped on the lower right-hand corner of the back cover. All of the edges are unstained and trimmed. This edition has buff end papers. Issued in a blue and white dust jacket printed in white and black. Originally priced at 6s., with a current price range estimated at between $15 and $35. Copies of this edition are hard to locate. *References:* GP-A25b, BM-191, CBI, NUC.

d. [New York]: Bantam Books, [1947]. 118p.
(First Bantam Books Paperback Edition, No. 131) Published in December of 1947. This edition is illustrated with stills from the RKO motion picture directed by Emilio Fernandez. All of the edges are stained red and trimmed. Originally priced at 25¢, with a current price range estimated at between $15 and $35. Copies of this edition are scarce. *References:* GP-A25d, BM-192, NUC, SRC, BRL.

e. [Rome]: Albatross Books, c1949. ?p.
(First Albatross Books Edition) Not seen. Original price unknown. The current price range is estimated at between $50 and $100. Copies of this edition are very scarce. *Reference:* GP-A25e.

f. Eliot, George, *pseud.*, i.e. Marian Evans, *afterwards* Cross, 1819–1880. *Silas Marner*, by George Eliot. *The Pearl*, by John Steinbeck. Edited by Jay E. Greene. New York: Noble and Noble, [1953]. 451p.

(Noble's Comparative Classics Edition) Not seen. Originally priced at $1.56, with a current price range estimated at between $20 and $40. Copies of this edition are difficult to obtain. *References:* GP-A25f, NUC, CBI.

g. London: Pan Books, [1954]. 157p.
(Pan Books Paperback Edition, No. 279) Not seen. Published on March 19, 1954. Combined with *Burning Bright*. Originally priced at 2s., with a current price range estimated at between $15 and $30. Copies of this edition are difficult to find. *References:* GP-A25g, EC, RC, WCBL, NUC.

h. London: Heinemann Educational Books, [1954]. 104p.
(New Windmill Series Edition) Not seen. Published in October of 1954 for use in schools. Illustrated by Vera Jarman. Originally priced at 4s., with a current price range estimated at between $20 and $45. Copies of this edition are scarce. *References:* GP-A25h, BNB, NUC.

i. Toronto: Macmillan, [1958]. 122p.?
(Second Canadian Edition) Not seen. Includes notes by R.L. Hale and P.A. deSouza for classroom use. Contains illustrations by José Clemente Orozco. Issued in decorative boards apparently without a dust jacket. Original price unknown. The current price range is estimated at between $30 and $90. Copies of this edition are difficult to obtain. *Reference:* BM-193.

j. Fuller, Edmund, 1902– *Four Novels for Appreciation*. New York: Harcourt Brace, [1960]. 666p.
(Combined Edition) Not seen. Prefaces and afterwords by Edmund Fuller. Study questions by Blanche Jennings Thompson. Includes: *Jane Eyre*, by Charlotte Brontë; *Kim*, by Rudyard Kipling; *Night Flight*, by Antoine de Saint-Exupéry; and *The Pearl*, by John Steinbeck. Originally priced at $3.36, with a current price range estimated at between $15 and $40. Copies of this edition are difficult to locate. *References:* CBI, NUC.

k. New York: Bantam Books, [1962]. 118p.
(A Bantam Pathfinder Edition, No. EP78) Not seen. Originally priced at 45¢, with a current price range estimated at between $4 and $8. Copies of this edition are relatively common. *References:* BIP, NUC.

l. Toronto: Macmillan, [1963]. ?p.
(Canadian Combination Edition) Not seen. Combined with *The Red Pony*. Illustrated by José Clemente Orozco. Apparently issued without a dust jacket. Original price unknown. The current price range is estimated at between $20 and $50. Copies of this edition are difficult to find. *References:* GP-A25i, BM-194.

m. [Moscow]: High School Publishers, 1964. ?p.
(First English-Russian Edition) Not seen. Published for the use of Russian students with a vocabulary at the back of the volume. Original price unknown. The current price range is estimated at between $35 and $65. Copies of this edition are extremely rare. *References:* GP-A25j, BM-195.

n. New York: The Viking Press, [1965]. 181p.
(New Completely Reset Edition) Not seen. Probably issued without a dust jacket. Includes the illustrations by José Clemente Orozco. Combined with *The Red Pony* with illustrations by Wesley Dennis. Originally priced at $3, with a current price range estimated at between $10 and $20. Copies of this edition are still fairly common. *References:* GP-A25k, CBI, BIP, NUC.

o. New York: The Viking Press, [1965]. 181p.
(Compass Books Paperback Edition, No. C177) Not seen. Also combined with *The Red Pony* with illustrations as indicated in **n.** above. Originally priced at $1.25, with a current price range estimated at between $5 and $10. Copies of this edition are fairly common. *References:* GP-A25l, CBI, BIP, NUC.

p. New York: Franklin Watts, [c1966]. 122p.
(Large Type Edition, "A Keith Jennison Book") Not seen. Later printings noted. Originally priced at $6.95, with a current price range estimated at between $25 and $50. Copies of this edition are difficult to find. *References:* GP-A25m, CBI, NUC.

q. London: Heinemann, 1967. 97p.
(A Reissue of the 1948 Edition) Not seen. Published on January 1, 1968 with the imprint date of 1967. Originally priced at 21s., with a current price range estimated at between $10 and $20. Copies of this edition are difficult to find. *References:* GP-A25n, BNB, CBI, BBIP, EC, NUC.

r. [Copenhagen: Grafisk Forlag, 1968]. 93p.
(Easy Reader Edition) Not seen. Apparently published in English and printed in Denmark by Grafisk Institut. Illustrated by Oskar Jorgensen. Original price unknown. The current price range is estimated at between $20 and $50. Copies of this edition are very difficult to obtain. *References:* GP-A25o, NUC.

s. London: Heinemann, [1969]. 97p.
(Probably a Reissue of the 1967 Reissue Edition) Not seen. Original price unknown. The current price range is estimated at between $5 and $15. Copies of this edition are difficult to find. *Reference:* GP-A25p.

t. Louisville, Ky.: American Printing House for the Blind, [1970]. ?p. (1v.)
(First Braille Edition) Not seen. Printed for the visually impaired. Original price unknown. No price range is estimated for this edition. Availability has not been determined. *Reference:* GP-A25q.

u. London: Pan Books, [1970]. ?p.
(First Pan Books Separate Edition) Not seen. Published in September of 1970 in paperback. Originally priced at 20s., with a current price range estimated at between $5 and $10. Copies of this edition are still somewhat difficult to obtain in the United States. *References:* BM-196, BBIP, WCBL.

v. [London]: Distributed by Heron Books, [1971]. 308p.
(Heron Uniform Edition) Combined with *To a God Unknown*. Published in the Heron uniform imitation leather binding. Original illustrations by David W. Whitfield. Original price unknown. The current price range is estimated at between $100 and $200. Copies of this edition are scarce. *References:* GP-A25r, CBI, NUC, SRC.

w. Paine, Michael John. *The Pearl.* [By] John Steinbeck; retold by M.J. Paine. London: Heinemann Educational Books, 1974. 72p.
(Heinemann Guided Readers Edition, No. 8) Not seen. Published in July of 1974 in paperback and illustrated by Clifford Bayly. Originally priced at 35s., with a current price range estimated at between $5 and $10. Copies of this edition are relatively common. *References:* BNB, BBIP, WCBL.

x. [Harmondsworth, Eng., New York]: Penguin Books, [1976]. 181p. (First Penguin Combined Paperback Edition) Not seen. Combined with *The Red Pony. The Pearl* is illustrated by José Clemente Orozco and *The Red Pony* by Wesley Dennis. Originally priced at $1.50, with a current price range estimated at between $4 and $10. Copies of this edition are quite common. *References:* BM-198, NUC, CBI, BNB.

39. *The Pearl – Play* (1975)

Frost, Warren Lindsay. *John Steinbeck's The Pearl.* Dramatized by Warren Frost. Chicago: The Dramatic Publishing Company, [1975]. 76p.
(First and Only Separate Edition) Based on the novel with the same title. Bound in salmon-colored pictorial wrappers. Originally priced at $2.75, with a price range estimated at between $5 and $10. Copies of this edition are in print and rather common. *References:* NUC, SRC, BRL.

40. *Pipe Dream* (1956)

a. Rodgers, Richard. *Pipe Dream.* Book and Lyrics by Oscar Hammerstein II. Based on *Sweet Thursday* by John Steinbeck. New York: The Viking Press, 1956. 158p.
(First Edition) Published in May of 1956. Bound in fine silver cloth. Lettering and decorations on the front cover and spine stamped in lavender, yellow and black. Printed with pink end papers in front and green end papers in the back, both with photographs of the original cast in their various roles. Issued in a colored pictorial dust jacket depicting a scene from the stage production. The jacket design is by Bill English and the sketch of the palace flophouse scene ©1955 by Jo Mielziner. Variant copies have been noted with green end papers in the front and pink in the back with photographs of the original cast. There is probably no priority between issues. Originally priced at $3.50, with a current price range estimated at between $30 and $50. Copies of this edition are scarce. *References:* GP-A33j, BM-232 & 233, CBI, NUC, SRC.

b. Toronto: Macmillan, [1956]. 158p.
(First Canadian Edition) Not seen. Published at the same time as the Viking Press edition. Original price unknown. The current

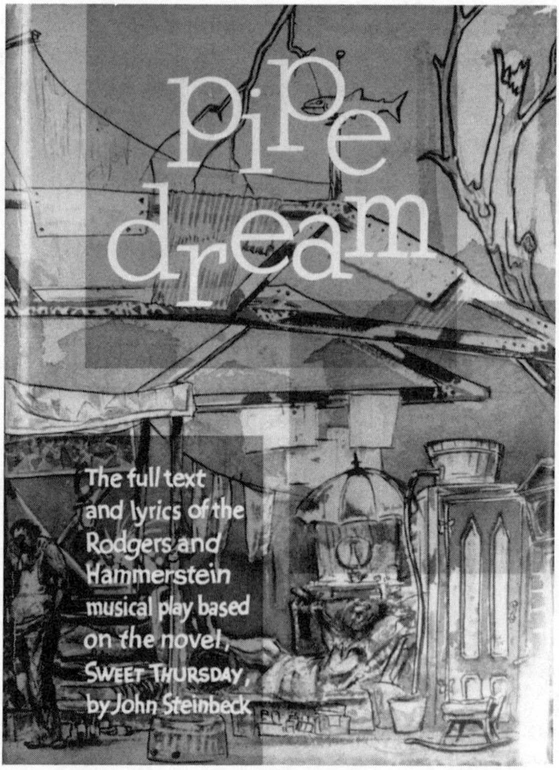

First edition of "Pipe Dream," with dust jacket designed by Bill English.

price range is estimated at between $25 and $40. Copies of this edition are very difficult to find. *Reference:* Viking.

41. *Positano* (1955?)

a. Salerno: Ente Provinciale per Il Turismo, [1955]. 30p. (First Italian Edition) Not seen. This account first appeared in *Harper's Bazaar* in May of 1953. Bound in stiff yellow wrappers. Lettering on the front, back and spine is printed in gold and black. A small drawing of Positano appears on the front cover printed in blue and brown. Original price unknown. The current price range is estimated at between $150 and $250. Copies of this edition are very scarce. *References:* GP-A34a, BM-235, NUC.

b. Salerno: Ente Provinciale per Il Turismo, [1959]. 30p.
(First English Language Edition) Also bound in stiff yellow wrappers. The lettering etc. is the same as the First Italian Edition. All of the edges are unstained and trimmed. "Steinbeck at Positano" appeared in the September 1964 issue of *L'Italia*, a review edited by Augusto Premoli and published in Rome by E.N.I.T. and by the Italian State Railways. In the Steinbeck Research Center at San Jose State University there is a copy which lists the publication date on page [2] as "1954" instead of "1959" as given in Goldstone/Payne (A34b). It is possible that copies listing "1959" as the publication date are a second issue (or even a second edition) of the English language version. Short of examining the printer's records, or publisher's files, it is virtually impossible to determine the priority of these variants. Original price unknown. The current price range is estimated at between $75 and $125. Copies of this edition are very difficult to locate. *References:* GP-A34b, NUC, SRC.

c. Salerno: Ente Provinciale per Il Turismo, [1959]. 30p.
(First French Language Edition) Not seen. This edition is identical to the Italian Language Edition with the following variants: at the bottom of the front cover the line "Assessorato Per Il Turismo Della Regione Compania" is omitted; on the back cover in slightly smaller type is printed: "Printed in Italy/ Ed. fr." There are further minor changes to the copyright page and the title page and the text is entirely in French. There is no acknowledgment as to who did the translating. Issued in stiff wrappers. The *National Union Catalog* lists a copy of this edition published in [1955] with the notation [Traduction de L. et G. Fauré]. It is possible that the Bradford Morrow copy is a reprint of the earlier edition, but again, there is no way to be certain. Original price unknown. The current price range is estimated at between $275 and $500. Copies of this edition are extremely rare. *References:* BM-237, NUC.

42. *The Red Pony* (1937)

a. New York: Covici-Friede Publishers, 1937. 81p.
(First Limited Edition) Published in September of 1937. The related short stories that make up this collection first appeared in the following periodicals: "The Red Pony I, The Gift" in *The North American Review*, November 1933; "The Red Pony II, The Great Mountains," in *The North American Review*, December 1933; "The Red Pony III, The Promise" in *Harper's Magazine*,

August 1937; and "The Leader of the People" in *Argosy* (London), August 1936. This edition is set in monotype Italian Oldstyle and printed on hand-made LaGarde paper. Six hundred and ninety-nine numbered copies were printed by the Pynson Printers of New York under the supervision of Elmer Adler. Each copy was signed by the author. Bound in beige cloth. The front cover, spine, and back cover are intersected by eight vertical and five horizontal gray rules. A rearing pony printed in red appears on the front cover in the second middle square from the top. In the third middle square just below the rearing pony in red is: M C M X X X V I I. The spine is printed in red vertically from the top: *JOHN STEINBECK THE RED PONY*. The top edges are trimmed and the others are untrimmed. Issued in a clear cellophane dust jacket and a tan publisher's case with the spine printed in black: *[ornament] THE/ RED/ PONY/ [ornament]/ No./ [in red manuscript]...* . Some copies were not numbered or signed. Also there exists an unrecorded lettered issue in the Valentine Collection. It is identical to the other copies of this edition except that instead of being numbered it is lettered "H" in red ink on the colophon and on the publisher's slipcase, where ordinarily one finds the limitation number. The colophon does not mention a lettered series, nor do Goldstone/Payne indicate the existence of lettered copies. Originally priced at $10, with a current price range estimated at between $500 and $800. The variant copies run as high as $2,500. Copies of this edition are very rare. *References:* GP-A9a, BM-78 through 80, NUC, CBI, SRC.

b. Toronto: McLeod, [1937]. 81p.
(First Canadian Edition) Not seen. Apparently published about the same time as the Covici-Friede limited edition. Originally priced at $12, with a current price range estimated at between $300 and $700. Copies of this edition are very rare. *References:* GP-A9e, CBI.

c. London: Chatto & Heinemann, [1940]. 253p.
(Evergreen Books Edition, No. 23) Not seen. Published in December of 1940 and combined with *Of Mice and Men*. Bound in stiff pink wrappers, gray spine with gray decorations on both front and back covers. In reverse printing within a gray oval enclosed by gray decorations: *OF MICE AND MEN/ [dot]/ THE RED PONY/ [ornament]/* John Steinbeck. The spine is printed in reverse vertically from top to bottom: *OF MICE AND MEN & THE RED PONY*— John Steinbeck. All of the edges are unstained and trimmed. There are no end papers. Issued in a green and pink dust jacket. Originally

priced at 1s., with a current price range estimated at between $5 and $20. Copies of this edition are scarce. *References:* GP-A7m & A9b, EC, CBI.

d. New York: The Viking Press, 1945. 131p.
(First Illustrated Edition) Published in September of 1945. Set in Monotype Emerson and Bernhard Modern types with water-color illustrations by Wesley Dennis. Bound in coarse beige cloth. A colored illustration on a blue background is pasted off-center on the front cover, enclosed within a wide blue border. The spine is stamped in gold on a blue background vertically from top to bottom: *JOHN STEINBECK The Red Pony THE VIKING PRESS.* All of the edges are trimmed. Has end papers with a colored illustration of horses running. Issued in a publisher's blue-gray paperboard case with a paper label printed on the front. Two major variants have been noted: (1) Bound in fine beige cloth. This variant was printed by the Zeese-Wilkinson Company and bound by H. Wolff Book Manufacturing Company. It was issued in a blue-gray publisher's paperboard case. (2) Bound in fine beige cloth. This variant was printed by Rogers-Kellogg-Stillson and bound by the Kingsport Press. This variant was issued in a tan publisher's paperboard case. Originally priced at $5, with a current price range estimated at between $35 and $75. Each of these variants still seems to be relatively common. *References:* GP-A9c, BM-81, MB-28, NUC, CBI, SRC, BRL.

e. New York: The Viking Press, 1945. 131p.
(Book-of-the-Month Club Edition) Not seen. Published as a dividend for the Club in September of 1945. Original price unknown. The current price range is estimated at between $10 and $25. Copies of this edition appear to be fairly common. *References:* GP-A9f, Bantam.

f. Toronto: Macmillan, [1945]. 131p.
(First Canadian Illustrated Edition) Not seen. Published at the same time as the Viking Press edition. Originally priced at $6.50, with a current price range estimated at $15 and $40. Copies of this edition are difficult to locate. *References:* GP-A9g, CBI.

g. Tokyo: Nan'un-do, [c1945]. 142p.
(Nan'un-do's Contemporary Library Edition) Not seen. Edited with notes by Kyuichiro Machida and Chuichi Sugiyama. The preface and notes are in Japanese. The *National Union Catalog* lists a later printing issued in [1954]. Original price unknown. The

current price range is estimated at between $20 and $50. Copies of this edition are scarce. *References:* GP-A9h, NUC.

h. Cleveland: World Publishing Company, [1948]. 303p.
(Forum Books Edition, No. F188) Not seen. This edition, published in April of 1948, includes the stories contained in *The Long Valley* under the title ... *The Red Pony and Other Stories*. The dust jacket designed by Leo Manso illustrates scenes from the movie. Originally priced at 49¢, with a current price range estimated at between $15 and ¢25. Copies of this edition are difficult to find. *References:* GP-A9i, BM-82, CBI, NUC.

i. New York: Bantam Books, [1948]. 117p.
(First Bantam Books Paperback Edition, No. 402) Published in August of 1948. Includes the short story "Junius Maltby" from *The Pastures of Heaven* on pages [91]–117. Originally priced at 25¢, with a current price range estimated at between $8 and $25. Copies of this edition are fairly difficult to find. *References:* GP-A9j, BM-83, MB-20, NUC, SRC, BRL.

j. London: William Heinemann Ltd., [1949]. 86p.
(First British Illustrated Edition) Not seen. Published in August of 1949 and illustrated with eight photographs from the film. Bound in stiff paper wrappers. Lettering on the front cover and spine is reverse printing on a red background. Printing and decoration on the back cover is in red. All of the edges are unstained and trimmed. Originally priced at 2s. 6d., with a current price range estimated at between $35 and $50. Copies of this edition are scarce. *References:* GP-A9d, EC, RC, WCBL.

k. New York: Bantam Books, [1955]. 120p.
(New Bantam Books Paperback Edition, No. 1406) Not seen. Also includes "Junius Maltby" from *The Pastures of Heaven*. Originally priced at 25¢, with a current price range estimated at between $4 and $8. Copies of this edition are difficult to find. *References:* NUC, BIP.

l. New York: The Viking Press, [1959]. 120p.
(A Reissue of the Illustrated Edition) Not seen. Includes the original drawings by Wesley Dennis. Issued in a reinforced library binding without a dust jacket. Originally priced at $2.75, with a current price range estimated at between $20 and $30. Copies of

this edition seem relatively scarce. *References:* GP-A9l, BM-85, CBI, BIP, NUC.

m. Louisville, Ky.: American Printing House for the Blind, [1959]. 1v. (First Braille Edition) Not seen. Original price unknown. No price range has been estimated for this edition. Availability has not been determined. *Reference:* GP-A9m.

n. London: Heinemann Educational Books, [1961]. 92p.
(New Windmill Series Edition) Not seen. Published in December of 1961, for use in schools. Illustrated by Robert Hodgson. Originally priced at 5s., with a current price range estimated at between $5 and $15. Copies of this edition are difficult to find. *References:* GP-A9n, BNB, BBIP.

o. Moscow: [No Publisher Given], [1962]. ?p.
(First Russian Edition) Not seen. Published with text in English. Original price unknown. The current price range is estimated at between $20 and $40. Copies of this edition are scarce. *Reference:* GP-A9o.

p. New York: Bantam Books, [1963]. 120p.
(A Bantam Books Pathfinder Edition, No. EP79) Published in February of 1963. Originally priced at 45¢, with a current price range estimated at between $4 and $8. Copies of this edition are relatively common. *References:* NUC, BIP.

q. Toronto: Macmillan, [1963]. 46, 122p.
(Canadian Combined Illustrated Edition) Not seen. *The Red Pony* is illustrated by Wesley Dennis and *The Pearl* is illustrated by José Clemente Orozco. Original price unknown. The current price range is estimated at between $15 and $35. Copies of this edition are difficult to find. *References:* GP-A9p, NUC.

r. Toronto: Macmillan, [1963]. 128p.
(Canadian Separate Illustrated Edition) Not seen. Illustrated by Wesley Dennis and includes study material prepared by C.J. Porter. Originally priced at $1.10, with a current price range estimated at between $15 and $35. Copies of this edition are hard to locate. *References:* GP-A9q, CBI.

s. Popp, Lilian M., ed. *Four Complete Heritage Novels*. New York: Globe Book Company, [1963]. 605p.

(Combined Edition) Not seen. Contains *The Red Pony*. Originally priced at $3.36, with a current price range estimated at between $15 and $25. Copies of this edition are difficult to find. *References:* NUC, CBI.

t. New York: The Viking Press, [1965]. 181p.
(Compass Books Paperback Edition, No. C177) Not seen. Combined with *The Pearl*; includes the illustration as in No. 17 above. Originally priced at $1.25, with a current price range estimated at between $5 and $10. Copies of this edition are fairly common. *References:* GP-A9r, CBI, BIP, NUC.

u. New York: Franklin Watts, [c1966]. 131p.
(Large Type Edition—"A Keith Jennison Book") Not seen. Originally priced at $6.95, with a current price range estimated at between $20 and $35. Copies of this edition appear to be difficult to locate. *References:* GP-A9s, CBI, NUC.

v. London: Transworld Publications, 1967. 120p.
(Corgi Books Paperback Edition) Not seen. Published in June of 1967. Originally priced at 3s. 6d., with a current price range estimated at between $5 and $10. Copies of this edition are hard to find. *References:* BNB, BBIP.

w. London: Heinemann, [1968]. 91p.
(Pyramid Books Edition) Not seen. Published in June of 1968. Published for adolescents. Originally priced at 15s., with a current price range estimated at between $10 and $25. Copies of this edition are difficult to find. *References:* GP-A9t, BNB, BBIP, CBI.

x. [Harmondsworth, Eng., New York]: Penguin Books, [1976]. 181p.
(First Penguin Combined Paperback Edition) Not seen. Combined with *The Pearl. The Red Pony* is illustrated by Wesley Dennis and *The Pearl* by José Clemente Orozco. Originally priced at $1.50, with a current price range estimated at between $4 and $10. Copies of this edition are quite common. *References:* BM-198, NUC, CBI, BNB.

43. *A Russian Journal* (1948)

a. New York: The Viking Press, 1948. 220p.
(First Edition) Published in April of 1948. Parts of this book first

appeared in *The New York Herald Tribune* from January 14, 1948 to January 31, 1948. Contains photographs by Robert Capa. Lettering and rules on the front cover and spine are printed in blue. The top edges are stained blue, and all edges are trimmed. Issued in a colored pictorial dust jacket. Four variant binding cloths have been noted for this edition. They are listed below in order of scarcity; however, no priority of issue has yet been determined:

1. Grayish-green cloth (near Centroid 150). Light grayish-yellowish-brown spine (near Centroid 79). Very rare.
2. Covers the same as 1. Grayish-yellow spine (near Centroid 90). Scarce.
3. Covers the same as 1. Moderately yellow spine. (near Centroid 89). Fairly common.
4. Light bluish-green cloth (near Centroid 163). Spine the same as 3. Most common.

Originally priced at $3.75, with a current price range estimated at between $125 and $300. Copies of this edition vary as to the bindings listed above. *References:* GP-A27a, BM-201 through 203, CBI, NUC, SRC.

b. Toronto: Macmillan, 1948. 220p.
(First Canadian Edition) Not seen. Published at the same time as the Viking Press edition. Originally priced at $4.50, with a current price range estimated at between $65 and $120. Copies of this edition are difficult to locate. *References:* GP-A27c, CBI.

c. [No Place of Publication]: Non-Fiction Book Club, 1948. ?p.
(Subscription Book Club Edition) Not seen. Published in March of 1948 according to Bantam Books, which, if true, would make this the first edition. This early publication date is uncertain. Original price is unknown. The current price range is estimated at between $50 and $100. Copies of this edition are scarce. *References:* GP-A27d, Bantam.

d. [New York: New York Herald Tribune Syndicate, 1948]. [44]p.
(Photographic Edition) Not seen. This publication apparently carries the photographs taken by Robert Capa for Steinbeck's *A Russian Journal*. Original price is unknown. The current price range is estimated at between $60 and $100. Copies of this edition are extremely rare. *Reference:* NUC.

e. London: William Heinemann Ltd., [1949]. 220p.
(First British Edition) Not seen. Published in April of 1949. Also

the SHORT REIGN
OF PIPPIN IV
A Fabrication
JOHN STEINBECK

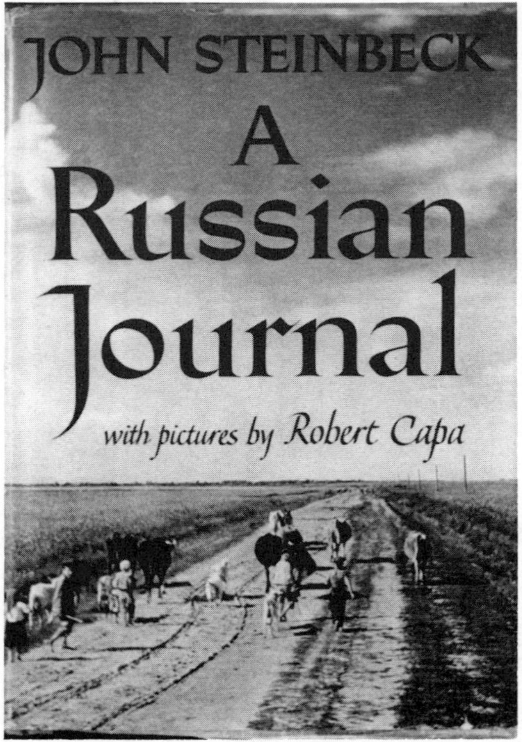
JOHN STEINBECK
A
Russian
Journal
with pictures by Robert Capa

includes the pictures by Robert Capa. Bound in blue cloth. The front cover is stamped in silver with a sketch outline of the Kremlin. Lettering and ornament on the spine are also stamped in silver. The Heinemann windmill is blind-stamped on the lower right-hand corner of the back cover. All of the edges are unstained and trimmed. Issued in a cream dust jacket printed in red, blue, brown, and green. Originally priced at 21s., with a current price range estimated at between $40 and $80. Copies of this edition are difficult to find. *References:* GP-A27b, EC, WCBL, CBI, NUC.

f. New York: Bantam Books, [1970]. 218p.
(First Bantam Paperback Edition, No. N4886) Published in May of 1970. Includes 65 photographs taken by Robert Capa. Originally priced at 95¢, with a current price range estimated at between $5 and $15. Copies of this edition can still be located, but are becoming more difficult to find. *References:* GP-A27e, BM-204, MB-75, BIP, BRL.

44. *Saint Katy the Virgin* (1936)

a. [New York: Covici-Friede, 1936]. 25[1]p.
(First Limited Edition) Issued as a Christmas gift for friends of the author and publisher. The text is a story later included in *The Long Valley* (1938). One hundred ninety-nine numbered copies were printed from Estienne type on Perusia handmade paper. Each copy was signed by the author. The actual printing was done by S.A. Jacobs, The Golden Eagle Press, Fleetwood, Mount Vernon, New York. Bound in decorated boards with a gold cloth spine. The spine is printed in red vertically from top to bottom: SAINT KATY THE VIRGIN. The top edges are trimmed, and the front and bottom edges are untrimmed. First issued in a glassine dust jacket. Some copies have a slip laid in, printed in red: MERRY/ CHRISTMAS/ *to the* FRIENDS OF/ COVICI•FRIEDE/ [star]/ WE HAVE THE HONOR/ TO ANNOUNCE FOR/ FEBRUARY PUBLICATION/ A NEW NOVEL/ BY JOHN STEINBECK/ *OF MICE AND MEN/* [star]/ Other books by John Steinbeck/ Published by Covici•Friede—/ *Tortilla Flat, In Dubious Battle,/ To a God Unknown, The Pas-/ tures of Heaven and The Cup/ of*

Opposite: (Left) First edition of "The Short Reign of Pippin IV," with dust jacket by William Pene duBois, who illustrated the book. (Right) First edition of "A Russian Journal" (in dust jacket).

Gold. Not for sale. The current price range is estimated at between $1,500 and $2,000. Copies of this limited edition are extremely rare. *References:* GP-A6a, BM-56, NUC, SRC, BRL (photocopy).

b. [New York: Covici-Friede, 1936] 25[1]p.
(Out-of-Series Edition) Not seen. In the Valentine Collection there is a signed but unnumbered, out-of-series copy. This copy also has a printed slip laid in which states: "Season's Greetings *[star]* Christmas 1937 *[star]* Covici•Friede." Otherwise this copy is identical to the numbered and signed issue. Not for sale. The current price range is estimated at between $2,500 and $3,500. Copies of this edition are extremely rare. *Reference:* BM-57.

45. *Sea of Cortez* With Edward F. Ricketts (1941)

a. New York: The Viking Press, 1941. 277p.
(First Edition, Issue in Wrappers) Published with the subtitle: *A Leisurely Journal of Travel and Research with a Scientific Appendix Comprising Materials for a Source Book on the Marine Animals of the Panamic Faunal Provence*. This issue actually is an advance copy and prints only the first half of the text, completely omitting the Scientific Appendix which appears in the regular trade cloth edition. A copy has been noted with a publisher's form letter dated November 17, 1941, announcing publication. This advance issue was probably released sometime in November of 1941. Bound in brown wrappers. All of the edges are unstained and trimmed. Some copies were issued in a publisher's paperboard box. Apparently there is a variant issue without a publisher's label on the front cover. Viking also issued a salesman's dummy which contains the first twelve pages of the text with the remainder of the leaves being left blank. It also includes several pages from the appendix. This dummy copy was issued in a binding differing from that of the regular trade edition, as well as variations in the title page design and layout of the text. The copyright page has been left blank, and following the title page is a statement regarding the illustrations: "There will be numerous half-tone illustrations in black and 15 in full color." This dummy copy has a dust jacket which has both the spine and front cover similar to the final published version, but leaves the rear panel and fly blank. Apparently not for sale. The current price range is estimated at between $1,500 and $2,500. Copies of this edition are very scarce. *References:* GP-A15a, BM-138 & 139, NUC, SRC.

b. New York: The Viking Press, 1941. 598p.
(First Edition, Issue in Cloth) Officially published on December 5, 1941. Bound in green cloth. The front cover is stamped in silver: Sea of Cortez/ A LEISURELY JOURNAL OF TRAVEL AND RESEARCH. The spine is stamped in silver: Sea of/ Cortez/ Steinbeck/ AND/ Ricketts/ THE VIKING PRESS. The top edges are stained orange. All of the edges are trimmed. A map of Lower California is printed in blue on both front and back end papers. Issued in a blue, orange, and white dust jacket printed in white, designed by W.V. Eckardt. Originally priced at $5, with a current price range estimated at between $150 and $300. Copies of this edition are becoming more difficult to find. *References:* GP-A15b, BM-140, MB-48, CBI, NUC, SRC.

c. Toronto: Macmillan, [1941]. 598p.
(First Canadian Edition) Not seen. Originally priced at $6.50, with a current price range estimated at between $75 and $125. Copies of this edition are difficult to locate. *References:* GP-A15c, CBI.

d. Mamaroneck, N.Y.: Paul R. Appel, 1971 [c1941]. 598p.
(Reprint Limited Edition) Published in a limited edition of 750 copies. The dust jacket for this edition was trimmed too short at the bindery and only a few copies were sent out before the publishers determined to issue it without the jacket. Originally priced at $20, with a current price range estimated at between $20 and $40. Copies of this edition still appear to be in print. *References:* GP-A15k, BM-143, BIP, NUC, SRC.

46. *The Short Novels of John Steinbeck* (1953)

a. New York: The Viking Press, 1953. 407p.
(First Edition) Published in September of 1953. Carries an introduction by Joseph Henry Jackson and the following short novels: *Tortilla Flat, The Red Pony, Of Mice and Men, The Moon Is Down, Cannery Row,* and *The Pearl*. The text is printed in double columns. Bound in brick-red cloth. The front cover is printed in black: *[ornament]* J S *[ornament]*. The spine is also printed in black: *[vertically] The Short Novels of/ [horizontally]* JOHN STEINBECK *[dot]/ [vertically] The/ Viking/ Press*. The top edges are stained yellow with the top and bottom edges trimmed, and the front edges untrimmed. Issued in a gray dust jacket printed in white, black, and orange. The Steinbeck Research

Center at San Jose State University has a variant copy with the date omitted from the title page. The spine is also different. It reads: *[horizontally] The Short Novels of/* JOHN STEINBECK/ *[dot]/ [vertically] The/ Viking/ Press*. Originally priced at $2.95, with a current price range estimated at between $20 and $40. Copies of this edition are difficult to find. *References*: GP-A30a, BM-209, CBI, NUC, SRC.

b. Toronto: Macmillan, [1953]. 407p.
(First Canadian Edition) Not seen. Published at the same time as the Viking Press edition. Originally priced at $3.50, with a current price range estimated at between $15 and $35. Copies of this edition are difficult to locate. *References:* GP-A30c, CBI.

c. Garden City, N.Y.: The Literary Guild of America, [1953]. ?p.
(Subscription Edition) Not seen. Apparently published for subscribers only. Original price unknown. The current price range is estimated at between $15 and $30. Copies of this edition are scarce. *Reference:* GP-A30d.

d. London: William Heinemann Ltd., [1954]. 568p.
(First British Edition) Published on March 15 of 1954. Several later printings have been noted. Bound in black cloth. Lettering and rules on the spine are stamped in gold and red. The Heinemann windmill is blind-stamped on the lower right-hand corner of the back cover. All of the edges are unstained and trimmed. Issued in a glassine dust jacket. Originally priced at 15s., with a current price range estimated at between $10 and $30. Copies of this edition are difficult to locate. *References:* GP-A30b, BNB, CBI, WCBL, EC, NUC, SRC.

e. New York: The Viking Press, [1963]. 527p.
(A New Completely Reset Edition) The text is not in double columns as was the first edition. Various states of binding and dust jackets have been noted for this edition. The priority of these has not been determined. Some copies have been noted in brown cloth and in gray cloth with a blue spine. A Book Club edition was also published in 1963 with the gray cloth and blue spine binding. The top edges are stained yellow and the top and bottom edges are trimmed with the fore edges rough trimmed. The dust jacket of the Book Club Edition, designed by Robert Hallock, bears the statement "Book Club Edition" at the bottom of the front flap. Another variant has been noted bound in red imitation cloth with a dust jacket printed in a slightly darker maroon and blue. Still another

variant has been noted bound in half brown imitation leather on the spine and with bright mustard-colored imitation leather covers, stamped in blue and silver. Has the same sheets as the other variants cited above. Possibly issued without a dust jacket, and it seems to be the typical New York trade publisher's misguided notion of a deluxe binding. Originally priced at $6, with a current price range estimated at between $7 and $15. Copies of this edition appear to be rather common. *References:* GP-A30e, BRL.

f. Toronto: Macmillan, [1963]. 527p.
(Second Canadian Edition) Not seen. Published at the same time as the Viking Press edition listed in No. 5 above. Originally priced at $7.50, with a current price range estimated at between $10 and $20. Copies of this edition are difficult to find. *Reference:* CBI.

47. *The Short Reign of Pippin IV, A Fabrication* (1957)

a. New York: The Viking Press, 1957. 188p.
(First Edition) Published in April of 1957. Bound in strawberry cloth with heraldic blind-stamping. Has a yellow cloth spine printed vertically from top to bottom in red: STEINBECK *[design]* THE SHORT REIGN OF PIPPIN IV *[design]* VIKING. The top edges are stained red and all edges are trimmed. Issued in a colorful dust jacket printed in red, yellow, and black designed by the book's illustrator William Pene duBois. Originally priced at $3, with a current price range estimated at between $20 and $75. Copies of this edition still seem fairly easy to obtain. *References:* GP-A36a, BM-240 & 241, MB-86, CBI, NUC, SRC.

b. Toronto: Macmillan, 1957. 188p.
(First Canadian Edition) Not seen. Published at the same time as the Viking Press edition. Originally priced at $3.25, with a current price estimated at between $15 and $35. Copies of this edition are difficult to find. *References:* GP-36c, CBI.

c. London: William Heinemann Ltd., [1957]. 164p.
(First British Edition) Not seen. Published on May 27, 1957. Bound in blue cloth. Lettering on the spine is stamped in silver. The Heinemann windmill is blind-stamped on the lower right-hand corner of the back cover. All of the edges are trimmed. Issued in a decorative dust jacket printed in yellow, black, and red, designed by Osbert Lancaster. A variant binding has been noted in red cloth.

Originally priced at 12s. 6d., with a current price range estimated at between $25 and $45. Copies of this edition are difficult to obtain. *References:* GP-A36b, BM-242, CBI, NUC, BNB, EC, WCBL.

d. New York: The Viking Press, 1957. 188p.
(Book-of-the-Month Club Edition) Published in May of 1957. Printed by the Kingsport Press and there is a dot blind-stamped on the lower right-hand corner of the back cover. Also the dust jacket does not give the price and adds "Book-of-the-Month Club Selection" at the top of the front flap. Original price unknown. The current price range is estimated at between $6 and $10. Copies of this edition are fairly common. *References:* GP-A36d, BM-243, SRC, BRL.

e. New York: Books Abridged, [1957]. ?p.
(Combined Abridged Edition) Not seen. This abridgment was published in October of 1957 together with abridged versions of Gerald Durrell's *My Family and Other Animals* and two other short novels by Frances Parkinson Keyes and Weldon Hill respectively. Original price unknown. The current price range is estimated at between $35 and $75. Copies of this edition are scarce. *References:* GP-A36e, BM-244.

f. New York: The Viking Press, 1957. 188p.
(Variant Book-of-the-Month Club Edition) In this variant edition no printer is indicated and in its place is the statement: "Printed in the United States of America." There is the distinctive dot on the lower right-hand corner of the back cover. Original price unknown. The current price range is estimated at between $30 and $70. Copies of this edition are fairly common. *References:* GP-A36f, SRC.

g. New York: Bantam Books, [1958]. 151p.
(First Bantam Books Paperback Edition, No. A1753) Published in April of 1958. Originally priced at 35¢, with a current price range estimated at between $5 and $10. Copies of this edition are difficult to find. *References:* GP-A36g, BM-245, MB-89, BIP, BRL.

h. London: Pan Books, [1959]. 158p.
(First Pan Books Paperback Edition, No. G252) Not seen. Published on June 12, 1959. Originally priced at 2s. 6d., with a cur-

rent price range estimated at between $5 and $10. Copies of this edition are difficult to locate. *References:* GP-A36h, BNB, EC, BBIP.

i. [Harmondsworth, Eng., New York]: Penguin Books, [1977]. 151p. (First Penguin Books Paperback Edition) Published with a new cover design by Neil Stuart. Originally priced at 70s. and $1.95, with a current price range estimated at between $5 and $10. Copies of this edition are quite common. *References:* NUC, BNB, BIP, CBI.

48. *Speech Accepting the Nobel Prize for Literature* (1962)

a. New York: The Viking Press, [1962 or 3]. 10, [1]p.
(First and Only Separate Edition) Published in an edition consisting of three thousand two hundred copies for friends of the author and publisher. Printed by the Meriden Gravure Company and the Spiral Press in Emerson type on Mohawk Superfine paper. Bound in buff paper wrappers with large front and back inner folds. The wrappers enclose, but are not fastened to, the stapled sheets. Printed on the front cover in red: ACCEPTANCE SPEECH/ *[reverse printing on a red background]* JOHN STEINBECK/ THE NOBEL PRIZE/ FOR LITERATURE/ *1962*. All of the edges are trimmed. Not for sale. The current price range is estimated at between $50 and $125. Copies of this edition are difficult to locate. *References:* GP-A40a, BM-269, NUC, SRC, BRL (photocopy).

b. *Les Prix Nobel en 1962*. Stockholm: Imprimerie Royale P.A. Norstedt & Söner, [1963]. ?p.
(Combined Edition) The text of the speech is found on pages 50–55. Original price unknown. The current price range is estimated at between $20 and $40. Copies of this edition are scarce. *References:* NUC, SRC, BRL (photocopy).

c. "To the Swedish Academy." *Story*, Vol. 36, Issue 2, No. 139 (March–April 1963): 6–8.
(First Periodical Appearance) Originally priced at 50¢, with a current price range estimated at between $15 and $30. Copies of this periodical are very scarce. *References:* SRC, BRL (photocopy).

d. New York: Alexis Gregory and C R M (Del Mar, California), [1971]. 375p.

(First Nobel Prize Library Edition) Published under the sponsorship of the Nobel Foundation and the Swedish Academy. Combined with Faulkner and O'Neill. Contains the "Acceptance Speech" on pages 205–207. Original price unknown. The current price range for this volume is estimated at between $15 and $25. Copies of this edition are still relatively easy to find. *References:* GP-B175, BM-55, NUC, SRC, BRL.

e. "Nobel Prize Acceptance Speech by John Steinbeck." *A Supplement to the Book-of-the-Month Club News*, [No volume or date given], [4 unnumbered pages].
(Second Periodical Appearance) Page [4] lists a number of Steinbeck titles offered as dividends by the Book-of-the-Month Club. This version of the speech was probably published sometime in 1963. Issued to members of the Club. The current price range is estimated at between $10 and $20. Copies of this edition are very scarce. *References:* SRC, BRL (photocopy).

49. *Steinbeck: A Life in Letters* (1975)

a. New York: The Viking Press, [1975]. 906p.
(First Edition, Limited Issue) Published in a limited edition of 1,000 copies edited by Elaine Steinbeck and Robert Wallsten. The limited issue includes a facsimile of a letter bound in at the front of the book, which is omitted from the trade issue. Bound in dark blue buckram. The front cover is stamped in gold script: *Steinbeck*. The spine is stamped in gold within a light blue panel: STEINBECK/ *A Life in/* LETTERS/ *[light blue rule]/ Edited by/ Elaine Steinbeck/ and/ Robert Wallsten/ [in light blue]* VIKING. All of the edges are unstained with the top edges trimmed and the fore and bottom edges untrimmed. Has heavy light blue textured end papers. Issued in a heavy light blue publisher's slip case. Originally priced at $35, with a current price range estimated at between $45 and $75. Copies of this edition are still relatively easy to find. *References:* BM-280, CBI, SRC.

b. New York: The Viking Press, [1975]. 906p.
(First Edition, Regular Trade Issue) Bound in coarse black cloth. The front cover is stamped in silver and in script: *Steinbeck*. The spine has the following in reverse printing on a light blue panel: STEINBECK/ *A Life in/* LETTERS/ *[light blue rule below the*

panel]/ [in silver] Edited by/ Elaine Steinbeck/ and/ Robert Wallsten/ [in light blue] VIKING. The top edges are unstained and trimmed, while the fore and bottom edges are untrimmed. Has dark blue end papers. Issued in a black dust jacket printed in blue, white and lavender designed by Mel Williamson. Originally priced at $15, with a current price range estimated at between $15 and $30. Copies of this edition are quite common. *References:* NUC, BM-281, CBI, SRC, BRL.

c. Toronto: Macmillan, [1975]. 906p.
(First Canadian Edition) Not seen. Published at the same time as the Viking Press edition. Original price unknown. The current price range is estimated at between $15 and $30. Copies of this edition appear to be difficult to locate. *References:* Viking, CBIP.

d. London: William Heinemann Ltd., [1975]. 906p.
(First British Edition) The copyright page lists the publication date as [1975]; however, *British Books in Print* indicates that this edition was issued in January of 1976. Bound in light blue cloth. The spine is stamped in light blue: STEINBECK/ *A Life in/ Letters/ [rule]/* ELAINE STEINBECK/ AND/ ROBERT WALLSTEN/ *Heinemann*. All of the edges are unstained and trimmed. Has white end papers of heavier stock than the text. Issued in a dark blue dust jacket printed in white, yellow, and blue designed by Bob Hook. Originally priced at £8, with a current price range estimated at between $15 and $30. Copies of this edition are fairly easy to obtain. *References:* CBI, BM-282, BBIP, SRC.

e. [Harmondsworth, Eng., New York]: Penguin Books, [1976]. 908p.
(First Penguin Paperback Edition) Carries a new wrapper design by Neil Stuart. Originally priced at $5.95, with a current price range estimated at between $7 and $15. Copies of this edition are quite common. *References:* NUC, CBI, SRC, BRL.

f. London: Pan Books, 1979. 906p.
(Picador Books Paperback Edition) Not seen. Published in August of 1979. Originally priced at £3.95, with a current price range estimated at between $5 and $6. Copies of this edition are fairly common. *References:* BNB, WCBL.

50. *The Steinbeck Pocket Book* (1943)

a. Philadelphia: The Blakiston Company; distributed by Pocket Books Inc., New York, [1943]. 308p.
(First Edition) The copyright page indicates that the first printing was in November of 1943 and that the book was published in December of 1943. Bound in stiff pictorial wrappers, with title and partial contents printed on the front cover. The items included were selected by Pascal Covici. The spine is printed vertically from top to bottom: *[in reverse]* ANTHOLOGY *[in black]* THE *Steinbeck* POCKET BOOK *[in reverse, horizontally] 243/ [publisher's device]*. Includes advertisements on the back cover. Has red end papers. All of the edges are stained red and trimmed. Some copies vary a few centimeters in size. Originally priced at 25¢, with a current price range estimated at between $15 and $40. Copies of this edition are becoming scarce. *References:* GP-A21a, BM-171, SRC, BRL.

b. New York: Pocket Books, [1945]. 308p.
(Second Paperback Edition) Not seen. Originally priced at 25¢, with a current price range estimated at between $15 and $40. Copies of this edition are scarce. *Reference:* GP-A21b.

51. *Sweet Thursday* (1954)

a. New York: The Viking Press, 1954. 273p.
(First Edition, Issue in Wrappers) Not seen. This is an advance copy probably sent out before the announced June publication date. Originally announced with the title: *The Palace Flophouse*. Sewed and wrapped in the colorful pictorial dust jacket designed by Paul Galdone. On the rear panel of this wrapper is a Philippe Halsman photograph of Steinbeck. In this edition the end papers are included. The top edges are unstained and all of the edges are trimmed. Not for sale. The current price range is estimated at between $125 and $200. Copies of this edition are very scarce. *References:* GP-A33a, BM-226.

b. New York: The Viking Press, 1954. 273p.
(First Edition, Regular Trade Issue in Cloth) Published on June 10, 1954. Bound in beige cloth. Front cover printed: *[in blue, silhouette of bird]/ [in blue, silhouette of bird]/ [in red] Sweet Thursday/ [in blue, silhouette of bird]*. The spine is printed in red: JOHN/ STEINBECK/ *[in blue, silhouette of bird]/ Sweet/ Thursday/ [in*

First edition, regular trade issue, of "Sweet Thursday." Dust jacket shown was designed by Paul Galdone.

blue, silhouette of bird]/ THE/ VIKING PRESS. The top edges are stained red and all edges are trimmed. Issued in a colorful pictorial dust jacket designed by Paul Galdone with a Philippe Halsman photograph of Steinbeck on the rear panel. Originally priced at $3.50, with a current price range estimated at between $35 and $90. Copies of this edition are still relatively easy to find. *References:* GP-A33b, BM-227, NUC, CBI, MB-82, SRC, BRL.

c. Toronto: Macmillan, 1954. 273p.
(First Canadian Edition) Not seen. Published at the same time as the Viking Press edition. Originally priced at $3.95, with a current price range estimated at between $25 and $75. Copies of this edition are difficult to find. *References:* GP-A33e, CBI.

d. London: William Heinemann Ltd., [1954]. 264p.
(First British Edition) Not seen. Published on October 21, 1954. Bound in green cloth. The spine is stamped in gold: *Sweet/ Thursday/ [short Oxford rule]/ JOHN/ STEINBECK/* HEINEMANN. The Heinemann windmill is blind-stamped on the lower right-hand corner of the back cover. All of the edges are unstained and trimmed. Issued in a colored pictorial dust jacket. Originally priced at 12s. 6d., with a current price range estimated at between $35 and $60. Copies of this edition are difficult to find. *References:* GP-A33c, NUC, BM-228, CBI, BNB, WCBL.

e. New York: The Viking Press, 1954. 273p.
(Variant Edition) This edition is possibly a second printing of the first cloth bound edition, also published in June of 1954. On the bottom of the copyright page below the publisher's device [a Viking ship] is the statement: "PRINTED IN U.S.A. BY H. WOLFF." The top edges are unstained and there is a red dot on the lower left-hand corner of the back cover. Originally priced at $3.50, with a current price range estimated at between $35 and $90. Copies of this edition are scarce. *References:* GP-A33d, BRL.

f. New York: The Viking Press, 1954. 273p.
(Book-of-the-Month Club Edition) Not seen. Published in August of 1954. Printed on thinner paper than the regular trade edition. The title page is printed entirely in black with no red. The publisher's device [a Viking ship] and the name of the printer are omitted from the copyright page. Also, the dust jacket adds blurbs beneath the Halsman photograph, which the regular trade edition does not. Original price unknown. The current price range is estimated at between $10 and $20. Copies of this edition are relatively common. *References:* GP-A33f, BM-229, Bantam.

g. London: Reprint Society, [1955]. 264p.
(British Reprint Edition) Not seen. Issued in a dust jacket. Original price unknown. The current price range is estimated at between $25 and $45. Copies of this edition are difficult to locate. *References:* GP-A33g, BM-230.

h. Chicago: Sears Readers Club, 1955. ?p.
(Subscription Edition) Not seen. Published in January of 1955. Original price unknown. The current price range is estimated at between $20 and $40. Copies of this edition appear to be hard to find. *References:* GP-A33h, Bantam.

i. New York: Books Abridged Edition, [1955]. ?p.
(Combined Abridged Edition) Not seen. Appeared in the periodical *Books Abridged* sometime in 1955. Published together with the abridged versions of Ellen Glasgow's *The Women Within* and two other novels. The text of *Sweet Thursday* is printed on pages 7–114. Bound in decorative paper boards with a black cloth spine. Original price unknown. The current price range is estimated at between $45 and $75. Copies of this edition are scarce. *References:* GP-A33i, BM-231, Bantam, NUC.

j. New York: Bantam Books, [1956]. 180p.
(First Bantam Books Paperback Edition, No. A1412) Published in January of 1956. Originally priced at 35¢, with a current price range estimated at between $5 and $25. Copies of this edition are scarce. *References:* GP-A33k, NUC, BM-234, MB-85, BRL.

k. London: Pan Books, [1958]. 206p.
(First Pan Books Paperback Edition, No. GP92) Published on April 18, 1958. Later printings have been noted. Originally priced at 2s. 6d., with a current price range estimated at between $5 and $15. Copies of this edition are difficult to locate. *References:* GP-A33l, BBIP, BNB, EC, SRC.

l. New York: Bantam Books, [1961]. 240p.
(Bantam Books Classic Edition, No. FC103) Published in July of 1961. Originally priced at 50¢, with a current price range estimated at between $2 and $5. Copies of this edition are relatively common. *References:* BIP, BRL.

m. London: Heinemann, [1966]. 264p.
(Heinemann Uniform Edition) Not seen. Published on June 20, 1966. Later reissues have been noted, for example see GP-A33m. Originally priced at 21s., with a current price range estimated at between $10 and $30. Copies of this edition are difficult to locate. *References:* NUC, BBIP, WCBL, EC.

n. New York: Bantam Books, [1970]. 240p.
(New Bantam Classic Edition, No. NC5449) Published in March

of 1970. Originally priced at 95¢, with a current price range estimated at between $4 and $7. Copies of this edition are fairly common. *References:* NUC, BIP, BRL.

o. [London]: Distributed by Heron Books, [1971]. 461p.
(Heron Uniform Edition) Combined with *Cannery Row* and illustrated by Peter Whiteman. Issued in the Heron uniform imitation leather binding. Original price unknown. The current price range is estimated at between $100 and $200. Copies of this edition are very difficult to find. *References:* GP-A33n, NUC, CBI, SRC.

p. [Harmondsworth, Eng., New York]: Penguin Books, 1979. 273p.
(First Penguin Paperback Edition) Carries a new wrapper design by Neil Stuart. Originally priced at $2.25, with a current price range estimated at between $5 and $10. Copies of this edition are quite common. *References:* NUC, CBI, BRL.

52. *Their Blood Is Strong* (1938)

a. San Francisco, Calif.: Simon J. Lubin Society of California, Inc., 1938. 33, [34–36]p.
(First Edition, First Issue) Published in April of 1938. Printed on glossy slick paper and bound in slick black and white wrappers. Printed in reverse on the front are: "THEIR BLOOD IS STRONG"/ *by/* JOHN STEINBECK/ *25¢*. First appeared as a series entitled "The Harvest Gypsies" in *The San Francisco News* from October 5, 1936 to October 12, 1936. Originally priced at 25¢, with a current price range estimated at between $150 and $450. Copies of this issue are very scarce. *References:* GP-A10a, BM-16, NUC, SRC.

b. San Francisco, Calif.: Simon J. Lubin Society of California, Inc., 1938. 33, [34–36]p.
(First Edition, Second Issue) Included on the title page is the statement: "Second printing—May, 1938." Page [36] is left blank. Originally priced at 25¢, with a current price range estimated at between $50 and $90. Copies of this edition are scarce. *References:* GP-A10b, BM-86, SRC.

c. San Francisco, Calif.: Simon J. Lubin Society of California, Inc., 1938. 33, [34–36]p.
(First Edition, Third Issue) Not seen. Included on the title page is

the following statement: *"Second Printing—May, 1938/ Third Printing—June, 1938."* Page [36] that was left blank in the first and second issue now contains a list of sponsors. Originally priced at 25¢, with a current price range estimated at between $50 and $90. Copies of this issue are scarce. *Reference:* GP-A10c.

d. San Francisco, Calif.: Simon J. Lubin Society of California, Inc., 1938. 33, [34–36]p.
(First Edition, Fourth Issue) Included on the title page is the following statement: *"Second Printing—May, 1938/Third Printing—June, 1938/ Fourth Printing—December, 1938."* In this issue page [36] contains a list of sponsors revised from that of the third issue. Originally priced at 25¢, with a current price range estimated at between $35 and $75. Copies of this edition are scarce. *References:* GP-A10d, BM-88, SRC, BRL (photocopy).

e. In 1939 the Works Progress Administration (W.P.A.) published part of "Their Blood Is Strong" in pamphlet form as a throwaway prepared for a performance of "The Sun Rises in the West" at the Greek Theatre on the campus of the University of California at Berkeley, August 17, 1939. This pamphlet contains excerpts from the second chapter of this work. Not for sale. The current price range is estimated at between $150 and $225. Copies of this pamphlet are extremely rare. *Reference:* GP-A10e.

f. Logan, Iowa: The Perfection Form Company, [n.d., c1970?]. 32p.
(New Illustrated Edition) This is a new edition of this important pamphlet on Migrant workers in California. Originally priced at 95¢, with a current price range estimated at between $2 and $5. Copies of this edition are still in print. *References:* SRC, BRL.

53. *To a God Unknown* (1933)

a. New York: Robert O. Ballou, [1933]. 325p.
(First Edition, First Issue) Published in September of 1933. There were 1,498 copies printed, of which 598 were bound and sold. Bound in green cloth. The spine is stamped in gold: TO A GOD/ UNKNOWN/ STEINBECK/ ROBERT/ BALLOU. The top edges are stained black, and all of the edges are trimmed. Issued in a green pictorial dust jacket. The dust jacket, end papers, and vignette on the title page were designed by Mahlon Blaine. Originally priced at $2, with a current price range estimated at between $400 and $850.

Copies of this issue of the first edition are very rare. *References:* GP-A3a, BM-21, NUC, CBI, SRC.

b. New York: Covici-Friede Publishers, [1935?]. 325p.
(First Edition, Second Issue) This second issue is made up from the first issue sheets with a cancel title page, new binding and dust jacket. There is some confusion as to the date of publication. The *National Union Catalog* gives [1933], while Goldstone/Payne and Bradford Morrow give [1935]. The *Cumulative Book Index* (CBI) does not help clarify the situation by not listing the Covici-Friede issue at all. Bound in beige cloth. The front cover printed in green with a horizontal rule extending across the spine and back cover. The spine is printed in green: *[ornament]/* TO A GOD/ UNKNOWN/ *[rule]/* STEINBECK/ *[ornament]/* COVICI/ FRIEDE. The top edges are stained green, and the front edges are untrimmed, while the bottom edges are trimmed. Issued in a green and beige dust jacket. Originally priced at $2.50, with a current price range estimated at between $250 and $375. Copies of this issue of the first edition are scarce. *References:* GP-A3b, BM-23, NUC, SRC.

c. London: William Heinemann Ltd., [1935]. 268p.
(First British Edition) Not seen. Published in April of 1935. Bound in blue cloth. The spine is stamped in gold: *[double rule]/ [ornamental rule]/* TO A GOD/ UNKNOWN/ JOHN/ STEINBECK/ HEINEMANN/ *[ornamental rule]/ [double rule].* The Heinemann windmill is blind-stamped on the lower right-hand corner of the back cover. All of the edges are unstained and trimmed. Originally priced at 7s. 6d., with a current price range estimated at between $100 and $225. A cheaper edition is noted at 3s. 6d. Copies of this edition are very scarce. *References:* GP-A3c, NUC, CBI, EC.

d. Toronto: McLeod, [c1935]. 325p.
(First Canadian Edition) Not seen. Original price unknown. The current price range is estimated at between $90 and $150. Copies of this edition are scarce. *References:* GP-A3d, CBI.

e. Cleveland: World Publishing Company, [1943]. 247p.
(Tower Books Edition, No. T-204) Published in April of 1943. Issued in a pictorial dust jacket. Later reissues have been noted. Originally priced at 49¢, with a current price range estimated at between $15 and $25. Copies of this edition are becoming more difficult to locate. *References:* GP-A3f, BM-24, NUC, CBI, SRC.

f. New York: Dell Publishing Company, Inc., [circa 1949–1955]. 238p.
(Dell Paperback Edition, Nos. 358, 407, and 1407) The date of publication given on the verso of the title page as MCMXXXIII (1933) is only the publication date of the first edition, not the Dell edition. There were no Dell books published prior to 1943. The three variant issues of this Steinbeck title were probably published between 1949 and 1955. These are identical except for the numbers, advertisements in the back, and the color of the attached and free end papers. Issued in picturesque wrappers with a map of the area on the back cover. Originally priced at 25¢, with a current price range estimated at between $20 and $35. Copies of this edition are difficult to find especially No. 1407. *References:* GP-A3e, NUC, SRC, BRL.

g. New York: Bantam Books, [1955]. 181p.
(First Bantam Books Paperback Edition, No. A1324) Published in June of 1955. Issued in pictorial wrappers. Originally priced at 35¢, with a current price range estimated at between $7 and $20. Copies of this edition are somewhat difficult to locate. *References:* GP-A3g, BM-25, NUC, SRC, BRL.

h. London: Transworld Publishers, [1958]. 223p.
(First Corgi Books Paperback Edition, No. S487) Not seen. Published in February of 1958. Originally priced at 2s. 6d., with a current price range estimated at between $10 and $25. Copies of this edition are difficult to find. *References:* GP-A3h, BNB, EC.

i. [London: Transworld Publishers, 1966]. 221p.
(Corgi Modern Reading Edition, No. FL6755) Not seen. Published in April of 1966. There were seven separate Corgi book printings to 1963, of which this constitutes a new edition and varies from the earlier 1958 edition. Originally priced at 5s., with a current price range estimated at between $7 and $20. Copies of this edition are difficult to find. *References:* BM-26, BBIP, WCBL.

j. London: Heinemann, [1970]. 241p.
(A New Heinemann Edition) Not seen. Published in July of 1970. The pagination varies in some of the references cited below. This could be the result of several printings of this edition. Originally priced at £1.75, with a current price range estimated at between $15 and $35. Copies of this edition are difficult to obtain. *References:* GP-A3i, BBIP, CBI, WCBL, NUC.

k. [London]: Distributed by Heron Books, [1971]. 308p.
(Heron Uniform Edition) Combined with *The Pearl.* Contains original illustrations by David W. Whitfield. Issued in the Heron uniform imitation leather binding. Original price unknown. The current price range is estimated at between $100 and $200. Copies of this edition are scarce. *References:* GP-A3j, NUC, CBI, SRC.

l. Leicester, Eng.: F.A. Thorpe, [1974]. 331p.
(Ulverscroft Large Print Series Edition, Fiction) Not seen. Published in December of 1974. Originally priced at £1.50, with a current price range estimated at between $10 and $20. Copies of this edition are difficult to obtain; however, later printings are still in print. *References:* CBI, BNB, BBIP.

m. London: Pan Books, [1975]. 189p.
(Pan Books Edition) Not seen. Published in November of 1975. Originally priced at 50s., with a current price range estimated at between $5 and $10. Copies of this edition are fairly common. *References:* BNB, CBI, BBIP.

n. [Harmondsworth, Eng.; New York]: Penguin Books, [1976]. 181p.
(First Penguin Books Paperback Edition) Later printings noted. Originally priced at $1.50, with a current price range estimated at between $5 and $10. Copies of this edition are quite common. *References:* NUC, CBI, BNB, BRL.

54. *Tortilla Flat* (1935)

a. New York: Covici-Friede Publishers, [1935]. 316 [1]p.
(First Edition, Issue in Wrappers) First published in May of 1935. Approximately 500 copies were bound in wrappers. Possibly these were sent out in advance for review, etc., before the cloth bound issue but there is no evidence that this actually happened. This edition is illustrated by Ruth Gannett. Sewed and wrapped in the dust jacket. The top and bottom edges are trimmed, the front edges are rough trimmed. Not for sale. The current price range is estimated at between $500 and $1,000. Copies of this edition are very scarce. *References:* GP-A4a, BM-28, SRC.

b. New York: Covici-Friede Publishers, [1935]. 316 [1]p.
(First Edition, Issue in Cloth) Officially published on May 28, 1935,

in an edition of 4,000 copies. There were at least eight printings between May of 1935 and April of 1937. Illustrated by Ruth Gannett. Bound in tan cloth. The front cover is printed in blue with a horizontal rule extending across the spine and back cover. The lettering and ornaments on the spine are printed in blue. The top edges are stained blue and trimmed, while the front and bottom edges are rough trimmed. Issued in a beige pictorial dust jacket designed by Ruth Gannett that is printed in blue and black. Originally priced at $2.50, with a current price range estimated at between $350 and $750. Copies of this edition are scarce. *References:* GP-A4b, BM-29, NUC, SRC.

c. London: William Heinemann Ltd., [1935]. 313p.
(First British Edition) Not seen. Published in November of 1935. Bound in blue cloth. The lettering and rules on the spine are stamped gold. The Heinemann windmill is blind-stamped on the lower right-hand corner of the back cover. All of the edges are trimmed. Issued in a printed dust jacket. Originally priced at 7s. 6d., with a current price range estimated at between $325 and $700. Copies of this edition are very difficult to locate. *References:* GP-A4c, BM-31, NUC, CBI.

d. Toronto: McLeod, [c1935]. 316 [1]p.
(First Canadian Edition) Not seen. Originally priced at $2.50, with a current price range estimated at between $90 and $150. Copies of this edition are scarce. *References:* GP-A4e, CBI.

e. New York: The Modern Library, [1937]. 316 [1]p.
(The Modern Library of the World's Best Books Edition, No. 216) Published in September of 1937. Contains a Foreword by Steinbeck on pages [i–iii], which appears in this edition for the first time. Steinbeck apologizes for having written the book because "literary slummers have taken these people up [i.e., the *paisanos* who are characters in the book] with the vulgarity of duchesses who are amused and sorry for a peasantry." A number of variant dust jackets have been noted as well as a reinforced buckram binding. Originally priced at 95¢, with a current price range estimated at between $25 and $50. Copies of this edition are somewhat difficult to find. *References:* GP-A4f, BM-33, NUC, CBI, SRC, BRL.

f. Toronto: Macmillan, [1937]. 316 [1]p.
(Second Canadian Edition) Not seen. Originally priced at $1.10,

with a current price range estimated at between $25 and $50. Copies of this edition are difficult to locate. *Reference:* CBI.

g. New York: Grosset & Dunlap, [1937]. 316 [1]p.
(Novels of Distinction Series Edition) A reprint edition of the Covici-Friede first edition and contains the illustrations by Ruth Gannett. This particular reprint edition presents a bibliographic enigma. The date of publication is uncertain. The *Cumulative Book Index* (CBI) and the *National Union Catalog* (NUC) both list an edition first published in 1937 and another in 1945. The Steinbeck Research Center (SRC) at San Jose State University and the Bibliographic Research Library (BRL) both have a copy that gives only 1935 as the date of publication on the verso of the title page. This copy is bound in rust-colored cloth with a blue rule extending horizontally across the back cover, spine, and front cover. Lettering and ornaments on the spine are stamped in blue. The top edges appear to be stained green and all of the edges are trimmed. The dust jacket depicts Spencer Tracy, Hedy Lamar, and John Garfield from the movie version which premiered in 1942. Also stated on the dust jacket is "JOHN STEINBECK/ Author of/ THE GRAPES OF WRATH,/ THE MOON IS DOWN." This latter novel was not published until 1942. Additionally, on the inside front flap of the dust jacket and on the title page is a statement that the book was produced under wartime conditions. All of this leads me to suspect that there were at least two separate issues of this edition, one published in 1937 and another in 1945. The copies in SRC and BRL are probably the latter issue. This, of course, is merely conjecture. A 1951 edition is indicated by Bantam Books and also by Bradford Morrow (BM-36) as well as Goldstone/Payne (GP-A4o). I cannot verify this 1951 issue in any of the standard bibliographic sources. Publication dates for the Grosset & Dunlap reprint edition will have to remain a mystery until more authoritative information becomes available. Originally priced at $1, with a current price range estimated at between $15 and $35. Copies of this edition are hard to find and the first issue is very rare if it exists at all. *References:* GP-A4h, SN-34, NUC, CBI, SRC, BRL.

h. New York: P.F. Collier & Son Corporation, [c1940]. 316 [1]p.
(Collier Uniform Edition) Published in the uniform Collier binding of brown cloth with pictorial stamping in blue, maroon, and gold. Original price unknown. The current price range is estimated at between $20 and $40. Copies of this edition are difficult to obtain. *References:* GP-A4i, NUC, SRC, BRL.

i. Stockholm: The Continental Book Company, 1942. 316 [1]p. (Zephyr Books Edition, No. 7) Not seen. Original price unknown. The current price range is estimated at between $25 and $50. Copies of this edition are scarce. *References:* GP-A4j, NUC.

j. New York: Council on Books in Wartime, [circa 1943]. 192p. (Armed Services Edition, No. A-9) Published for consumption by the American military during World War II. Not for sale. The current price range is estimated at between $25 and $50. Copies of this edition are very difficult to locate. *References:* GP-A4k, MB-197, NUC, SRC, BRL.

k. New York: Penguin Books, [1946]. 180p. (First Penguin Books Paperback Edition, No. 599) Published in June of 1946. Illustrated by Ruth Gannett. Bound in pictorial wrappers with a new cover design by "Jonas." Originally priced at 25¢, with a current price range estimated at between $15 and $30. Copies of this edition are scarce. *References:* GP-A4l, BM-35, NUC, BRL.

l. New York: The Viking Press, [1947]. 213p. (New Illustrated Edition) Published in October of 1947. Illustrated by Peggy Worthington. Bound in beige cloth. There is a colored illustration pasted on a green background on the front cover. The lettering on the spine is printed in dark green. The top edges are stained green and all of the edges are trimmed. Has pictorial end papers in color. Issued in a colored pictorial dust jacket designed by the illustrator. Originally priced at $6, with a current price range estimated at between $50 and $110. Copies of this edition are difficult to find. *References:* GP-A4d, NUC, CBI, SRC, BRL.

m. Toronto: Macmillan, [1947]. 213p. (First Canadian New Illustrated Edition) Not seen. Published at the same time as the Viking Press edition. Originally priced at $7, with a current price range estimated at between $50 and $110. Copies of this edition are scarce. *References:* CBI, Viking.

n. Stockholm: The Continental Book Company, [1949]. 316 [1]p. (A Reissue of the 1942 Edition) Not seen. Original price unknown. The current price range is estimated at between $25 and $40. Copies of this edition are difficult to locate. *Reference:* GP-A4m.

o. Harmondsworth, Eng.: Penguin Books, [1950]. 223p.
(British Penguin Books Paperback Edition, No. 786) Not seen. Published in November of 1950. Originally priced at 1s. 6d., with a current price range estimated at between $15 and $30. Copies of this edition are difficult to obtain. *References:* GP-A4n, BNB, EC.

p. [New York]: The New American Library, [1952]. 180p.
(Signet Books Paperback Edition, No. 816) Not seen. This is apparently a reissue of the Penguin edition first published in June of 1946. Contains the illustrations by Ruth Gannett and a new cover illustration by Alan Henner. Later printings have been noted. Originally priced at 25¢, with a current price range estimated at between $15 and $25. Copies of this edition are scarce. *References:* BM-37, NUC, BIP.

q. New York: The Viking Press, [1963]. 179p.
(New Completely Reset Edition) Not seen. Probably issued without a dust jacket. Published in April of 1963. Originally priced at $4, with a current price range estimated at between $10 and $20. Copies of this edition appear to be difficult to find. *References:* GP-A4p, NUC, BIP.

r. New York: The Viking Press, [1963]. 179p.
(Compass Books Paperback Edition, No. C134) Not seen. Also published in April of 1963. Originally priced at $1.45, with a current price range estimated at between $5 and $15. Copies of this edition are relatively common. *References:* GP-A4q, NUC, CBI, BIP.

s. New York: Bantam Books, [1965]. 151p.
(First Bantam Books Paperback Edition, No. H3019) Published in June of 1965. Originally priced at 60¢, with a current price range estimated at between $4 and $15. Copies of this edition are relatively common. *References:* GP-A4r, BM-38, BIP, NUC, SRC, BRL.

t. London: Heinemann, [1967]. 317p.
(New Heinemann Edition) Not seen. Published on June 26, 1967. Later printings noted. Originally priced at 30s., with a current price range estimated at between $15 and $35. Copies of this edition are difficult to locate. *References:* GP-A4s, BNB, EC, BBIP, CBI.

u. [London]: Distributed by Heron Books, [1971]. 293p.
(Heron Uniform Edition) Issued in the Heron uniform imitation leather binding. Contains original illustrations by Paul Gaisford. Original price unknown. The current price range is estimated at between $100 and $200. Copies of this edition are very difficult to find. *References:* GP-A4u, NUC, CBI, SRC.

v. London: Heinemann Educational Books, [1973]. 146p.
(The New Windmill Series Edition, No. 175) Not seen. Apparently published for use in schools. Published in November of 1973. Contains illustrations. Originally priced at 45s., with a current price range estimated at between $10 and $25. Copies of this edition are difficult to locate. *References:* GP-A4u, BNB, WCBL. BBIP.

w. London: Pan Books, [1975]. 189p.
(First Pan Books Paperback Edition) Not seen. Published in October of 1975. Issued in pictorial wrappers. Originally priced at 50s., with a current price range estimated at between $5 and $10. Copies of this edition are somewhat difficult to find in the United States. *References:* BM-41, BNB, WCBL, BBIP.

x. Bath, Eng.: Lythway Press, [1975]. 284p.
(Large Print Edition) Not seen. Published in December of 1975. Originally priced at £4.05, with a current price range estimated at between $40 and $90. Copies of this edition are hard to find. *References:* BNB, CBI, WCBL, BBIP.

y. [Harmondsworth, Eng.; New York]: Penguin Books, 1971. 151p.
(New Penguin Reprint Edition) Not seen. Apparently a reprint of the 1947 Viking Press edition without the illustrations. Originally priced at $1.50, with a current price range estimated at between $5 and $10. Copies of this edition are still relatively common. *References:* BNB, CBI, NUC.

z. Franklin Center, Pa.: Franklin Library, 1977. 447p.
(Limited Edition) Not seen. Combined with *Of Mice and Men* and *Cannery Row*. Contains illustrations by Herbert Tauss. Part of the series: The Collected Stories of the World's Greatest Writers. Original price unknown. The current price range is estimated at between $50 and $90. Copies of this edition are difficult to locate. *References:* BM-42, NUC.

55. *Tortilla Flat—Play* (1937)

Kirkland, Jack. *Tortilla Flat, A Play in Three Acts*. Based on the novel by John Steinbeck and dramatized by Jack Kirkland. New York: Covici-Friede Publishers, [1937]. ?p.
(First Play Edition) Not seen. Goldstone/Payne cite a salesman's dummy copy with text to page 8 located in the Stanford University Library. The *National Union Catalog* lists a typewritten copy [New York: 1938], located in the New York Public Library. This latter copy was apparently one of those used in the production at the Henry Miller Theater in New York on January 12, 1938. It is difficult at this writing to determine if Covici-Friede actually published an edition of this play. Original price unknown. The current price range is estimated at between $500 and $950. Copies of this edition are extremely rare if they exist at all. *References:* GP-A4g, NUC.

56. *Travels with Charley: In Search of America* (1962)

a. New York: The Viking Press, [1962]. 246p.
(First Edition) Published in July of 1962 with eleven printings noted up to 1963. Selections first appeared in *Holiday*, July 1961; December 1961; and February 1962. Bound in coarse bleached cloth. A drawing of a dog is stamped in red on the front cover. Lettering on the spine is printed in red and black. Issued in a decorative beige dust jacket printed in brown and black. This dust jacket was designed by Don Freeman and has a photograph of Steinbeck and Charley by Hans Namath on the back cover. The top edges are stained yellow and all of the edges are trimmed. Has decorative end papers. There is a variant issue. This issue is smaller in size than the first issue and has "Winner of the 1962 Nobel Prize for Literature" statement on the dust jacket. The title page is printed completely in black. The copyright page does not have "Printed by Wolff Book Mfg. Co." statement and does not list any other printing other than "Published in 1962 by Viking Press." Originally priced at $4.95, with a current price range estimated at between $40 and $75. Copies of this edition are still fairly easy to find. *References:* GP-A39a, BM-262, MB-96 & 97, CBI, NUC, SRC.

b. Toronto: Macmillan, [1962]. 246p.
(First Canadian Edition) Not seen. Published at the same time as the Viking Press edition. Originally priced at $5.95, with a current

price range estimated at between $35 and $55. Copies of this edition are hard to locate. *References:* GP-A39d, CBI.

c. New York: The Viking Press, [1962]. 246p.
(Book-of-the-Month Club Edition) Published in August of 1962. There is a small brown square on the lower left-hand corner of the back cover on some copies while on others there is a small black dot. The statement "Book-of-the-Month Club Selection" is printed on the top of the front flap of the dust jacket and "BOOK-OF-THE-MONTH" on the lower part of the back flap. Original price unknown. The current price range is estimated at between $7 and $15. Copies of this edition are relatively common. *References:* GP-A39c, BM-265, BRL.

d. London: William Heinemann Ltd., [1962]. 246p.
(First British Edition) Published on September 17, 1962. Bound in blue cloth. Lettering and ornament on the spine are stamped in silver. All of the edges are unstained and trimmed. Issued in a red, white and blue pictorial dust jacket designed by Arnold Schwartzman. The back cover carries a photograph of Steinbeck and Charley. Originally priced at 21s., with a current price range estimated at between $40 and $90. Copies of this edition are scarce. *References:* GP-A39b, BM-264, NUC, CBI, BNB, BBIP, EC, SRC.

e. New York: The Viking Press, [1962]. 246p.
(*Better Homes and Gardens* Family Book Service Edition) This edition is identical to the Book-of-the-Month Club edition except that the statement of the Book Club edition is replaced by that of *Better Homes and Gardens.* Also the binding is half brown cloth on the spine and pale tan boards instead of full cloth. Lettering on the spine is printed in black. There is a drawing of a dog in brown on the lower right-hand corner of the front cover. All of the edges are unstained and trimmed. Original price unknown. The current price range is estimated at between $50 and $80. Copies of this edition are very scarce. *References:* BM-266, SRC (without dust jacket).

f. New York: Bantam Books, [1963]. 275p.
(First Bantam Books Paperback Edition, No. S2581) Published in July of 1963. Originally priced at 75¢, with a current price range estimated at between $5 and $10. Copies of this edition are scarce. *References:* GP-A39c, BIP, NUC, SRC, BRL.

g. London: Pan Books, [1965]. ?p.
(First Pan Books Paperback Edition, No. M110) Not seen. Published on November 5, 1965. Originally priced at 5s., with a current price range estimated at between $5 and $10. Copies of this edition are scarce. *References:* GP-A39f, BBIP, WCBL.

h. New York: Franklin Watts, [1965]. 246p.
(Large Type Edition—"A Keith Jennison Book") Not seen. Originally priced at $6.95, and in a library binding for $4.95. The current price range is estimated at between $30 and $50. Copies of this edition are difficult to locate. *References:* GP-A39j, NUC, CBI, BIP.

i. New York: The Viking Press, [1969]. 246p.
(Compass Books Paperback Edition, No. C251) Not seen. Originally priced at $1.65, with a current price range estimated at between $5 and $10. Copies of this edition are difficult to find. *References:* GP-A39h, CBI.

j. [London]: Distributed by Heron Books, [1971]. 245 [1]p.
(Heron Uniform Edition) This edition is uniform with the others issued in this series except it does not include any illustrations. Issued in the original imitation leather binding with a yellow ribbon marker. Original price unknown. The current price range is estimated at between $100 and $200. Copies of this edition are very difficult to find. *References:* GP-A39i, BM-267, SRC.

k. London: Heinemann, 1973. 246p.
(Second Heinemann Edition) Not seen. Originally priced at £2.25, with a current price range estimated at between $10 and $30. Copies of this edition are somewhat difficult to find. *References:* BNB, CBI.

l. Harmondsworth, Eng.; New York: Penguin Books, 1980. 275p.
(First Penguin Paperback Books Edition) Not seen. Originally priced at $2.95 and 70s. respectively, with a current price range estimated at between $5 and $10. Copies of this edition are relatively common. *References:* NUC, CBI.

57. *Un Américain à New-York et à Paris* (1956)

a. Paris: René Julliard, [1956]. 154p.
(First Edition, Limited Issue) Not seen. Published in May of 1956.

Issued in a limited edition of only 30 numbered copies. Bound in Buff wrappers. The front cover is printed in black: UN AMERICAIN/ A NEW YORK/ ET A PARIS/ MCMLVI. The spine is also printed in black: JOHN/ STEINBECK/ UN—AME-/ RICAIN A/ NEW YORK/ ET A PARIS/ JULLIARD. Printed on the back cover is: EDITION ORIGINALE. All of the edges are trimmed. The translation into French was done by Jean-François Rozan. The text is printed on bleached white paper. Original price unknown. The current price range is estimated at between $2000 and $3000. Copies of this limited issue of the first edition are extremely rare. *References:* GP-A35a, BM-238.

b. Paris: René Julliard, [1956]. 154p.
(First Edition, Regular Trade Issue) Also published in May of 1956. Translated by Jean-François Rozan. The text is printed on cheaper paper than the limited issue above. Bound in yellow wrappers with large front and back inner folds. Printed on the front cover to the right of a man with a suitcase leaning against a lamppost with a STOP signaled: *[in red]* JOHN STEINBECK/ *[on a white background]* Un Américain/ à/ New York/ et à/ PARIS/ *[at bottom of front cover, in script]* Lars Bo./ JULLIARD. Lettering on the spine is printed in black. On the back cover is printed with a drawing: IMPRIME EN FRANCE 390 fr./ +T.L. Originally priced at 390 fr., with a current price range estimated at between $200 and $300. Copies of this edition are very scarce. *References:* GP-A35b, BM-239, NUC, SRC.

c. Paris: René Julliard. [c1965]. 154p.
(A Reissue of the 1956 Edition) Not seen. Translated by Jean-François Rozan. Possibly there have been a number of reissues of this title. Just how many is uncertain. Original price unknown. The current price range is estimated at between $100 and $200. Copies of this edition are scarce. *Reference:* NUC.

58. *Vanderbilt Clinic* (1947)

[New York: The Presbyterian Hospital, 1947]. [13]p.
(First and Only Edition) This publication was the third of a series of reports for the friends and supporters of the Hospital. Bound in printed wrappers with the cover serving as the title page. *[Title page cover in reverse printing]* VANDERBILT CLINIC/ By John Steinbeck/ *[photograph]*. The photographs contained in this publication were by Victor Keppler. Not for sale. The current price

range is estimated at between $175 and $250. Copies of this pamphlet are very scarce. *References:* GP-A24a, BM-187, NUC, SRC, BRL (photocopy).

59. *The Viking Portable Library Steinbeck* (1943)

a. New York: The Viking Press, 1943. 568p.
(First Edition) Published in July of 1943. The contents of this collection were selected by Pascal Covici. Bound in tan cloth. There is a drawing on the lower right-hand corner of the front cover printed in red. Lettering, ornaments and rules on the spine are also printed in red. All of the edges are stained red and trimmed. Issued in a pictorial dust jacket designed by I. Steinberg. Originally priced at $2, with a current price range estimated at between $30 and $75. Copies of this edition are very scarce. *References:* GP-A19a, BM-164, MB-58, CBI, NUC, SRC, BRL.

b. Toronto: Macmillan, [1943]. 568p.
(First Canadian Edition) Not seen. Published at the same time as the Viking Press edition. Originally priced at $2.75, with a current price range estimated at between $20 and $50. Copies of this edition appear to be extremely scarce. *References:* Viking, CBI.

c. New York: The Viking Press, 1946. 609p.
(Second Edition, Revised, with a New Title) Published in January of 1946 with the new title: *The Portable Steinbeck*. Contents of this enlarged edition were also selected by Pascal Covici along with an introduction by Lewis Gannett. There are also biographical and bibliographical notes. The dates given in the notes for the portable editions do not correspond with the dates that appear on the copyright pages of the books. Bound in tan cloth. Issued in a print dust jacket. Originally priced at $2, with a current price range estimated at between $15 and $30. Copies of this hardbound edition are scarce. *References:* GP-A19b, BM-165, MB-59, CBI, NUC, SRC.

d. New York: The Viking Press, 1946. 609p.
(Third Corrected Edition) Probably published shortly after the second revised edition above. Here the errors in the dates of publication of the portable editions have been corrected and a chapter added to the biographical and bibliographical notes.

Original price, price range, and availability are the same as above. *References:* GP-A19c, SRC.

e. Toronto: Macmillan, [1946]. 609p.
(Second Canadian Edition) Not seen. Published at the same time as the Viking Press second edition. Since this edition has not been examined it is not possible to tell if the errors in the second Viking edition were present in this second Canadian edition. Originally priced at $2.75, with a current price range estimated at between $50 and $100. Copies of this edition are very scarce. *References:* Viking, CBI.

f. London: William Heinemann Ltd., [1950?]. 408p.
(First British Edition, with a New Title) Not seen. Contents of this edition selected by Pascal Covici. The publication date given by two bibliographic sources is July of 1951. However, 1950 is given on the verso of the title page. Issued with the title: *The Steinbeck Omnibus*. Bound in light orange cloth, with a drawing of a farm worker in red on the lower right-hand corner of the front cover. Lettering on the spine is printed in red. All of the edges are unstained and trimmed. Issued in a colored pictorial dust jacket designed by I. Steinberg. Originally priced at 12s. 6d., with a current price range estimated at between $290 and $325. Copies of this edition are very scarce. *References:* GP-A19d, BM-166, BNB, CBI, NUC, EC.

g. *The Indispensable Steinbeck*. New York: Book Society, 1951. 609p.
(Book Society Edition) Not seen. The text of this edition is identical with the 1946 Viking Press edition of *The Portable Steinbeck*. Original price unknown. The current price range is estimated at between $50 and $125. Copies of this edition are difficult to locate. *References:* GP-A19f, NUC.

h. New York: The Viking Press, [1957, c1946]. 609p.
(First Viking Press Paperback Edition) The third printing of the 1946 edition, published sometime in 1957, was the first paperback issue of this Steinbeck collection. Originally priced at $1.25, with a current price range estimated at between $15 and $30. Copies of this particular printing are scarce. *References:* CBI, BIP, BRL (7th printing, June 1961).

i. New York: The Viking Press, [1971]. 692p.
(Fourth Edition, Revised and Enlarged) Published with a new introduction by Pascal Covici, Jr. Also a chronology is added to the extensively revised biographical and bibliographical notes. Originally priced at $5.95 in hard cover and $3.25 in wrappers. The current price range is estimated at between $10 and $20 for the hard cover and $5–$10 for the copy in wrappers. Both bindings are relatively common. *References:* GP-A19e, BM-167 & 168, CBI, NUC.

j. [Harmondsworth, Eng.: New York]: Penguin Books, [1976]. 692p.
(First Penguin Books Paperback Edition) Revised, selected, and introduced by Pascal Covici, Jr. Carries a cover design by Neil Stuart and a cover photograph by Joseph Marvullo. The insert photograph of Steinbeck on the front cover is from The Bettmann Archive. Originally priced at $4.95, with a current price range estimated at between $7 and $15. Copies of this edition are quite common. *References:* NUC, CBI, BIP, BRL.

60. *Viva Zapata!* (1953)

a. [Roma: Tip. Babuina; Dist. Edizioni Dell'ateneo, 1953]. 182p.
(First Edition) Not seen. Published as part of the series: Edizioni Filmcritica, No. 1. Contains an introduction by Giovanni Calendoli. Bound in blue and white wrappers. The front cover is printed in black: JOHN STEINBECK ELIA KAZAN/ VIVA ZAPATA!/ *Introduzione de Giovanni Calendoli/ [publisher's device]/* EDIZONI FILMCRITICA. All of the edges are trimmed. Issued in a dust jacket printed in blue and black. "Viva Zapata!" by Merle Miller was based on the screenplay written by John Steinbeck and appeared in *Argosy*, February 1952. Original price unknown. The current price range is estimated at between $200 and $375. Copies of this edition are very rare. *References:* GP-A31a, NUC.

b. New York: The Viking Press, [1975]. 150p.
(First Edition in English – Compass Books Paperback, No. C579) Edited by Robert E. Morsberger who also contributes an essay entitled: "Steinbeck's Zapata: Rebel versus Revolutionary." Bound in stiff black wrappers printed in red and white. The cover was designed by Mel Williamson. All of the edges are unstained and trimmed. Originally priced at $2.95, with a current price range

estimated at between $5 and $15. Copies of this edition are fairly common. *References:* BM-214, CBI, NUC, SRC, BRL.

c. Toronto: Macmillan, [1975]. 150p.
(First Canadian Edition) Not seen. Published at the same time as the Viking Press edition. Original price unknown. The current price range is estimated at between $25 and $50. Copies of this edition are difficult to find. *Reference:* Viking.

61. *The Wayward Bus* (1947)

a. New York: The Viking Press, 1947. 312p.
(First Edition) Published in February of 1947 in an edition of 100,000 copies. Bound in dark reddish-orange cloth (Centroid 38). The front cover is stamped in gold: The Wayward Bus/ BY JOHN STEINBECK/ *[blind-stamping of a bus on the front cover showing up lighter than the rest of the binding].* The spine is also stamped in gold: JOHN/ STEINBECK/ The/ Wayward/ Bus/ *[ornament]*/ THE VIKING PRESS. The top edges are stained green and all of the edges are trimmed. Issued in a colored pictorial dust jacket designed by Robert Hallock. Two variant bindings have been noted. The first is browner than Centroid 38, with the blind-stamped bus on the front cover being darker than the rest of the binding. The second is pinker than Centroid 38, with the blind-stamped bus on the front cover being the same shade as the rest of the binding. Originally priced at $2.75, with a current price range estimated at between $25 and $75. Copies of this edition are still fairly easy to locate. *References:* GP-A23a, BM-181, CBI, NUC, SRC, BRL.

b. Toronto: Macmillan, 1947. 312p.
(First Canadian Edition) Not seen. Originally priced at $3, with a current price range estimated at between $15 and $35. Copies of this edition are difficult to find. *References:* GP-A23d, CBI.

c. New York: The Viking Press, 1947. 312p.
(Book-of-the-Month Club Edition) Published in March of 1947. Issued in unglazed cloth with the top edges unstained and a blind-stamped dot on the lower left-hand corner of the back cover. This edition was printed by the Kingsport Press and variant copies by H. Wolff. Original price unknown. The current price range is estimated at between $15 and $45. Copies of this edition are fairly

common. *References:* GP-A23c, BM-184 & 185, SRC, BRL, Bantam.

d. New York: Council on Books in Wartime, [1947]. 256p.
(Armed Services Edition, No. 1232) Not seen. Published in April of 1947. Published for consumption by the American military during World War II. Not for sale. The current price range is estimated at between $20 and $50. Copies of this edition are very scarce. *References:* GP-A23e, NUC, Bantam.

e. In *Omnibooks Magazine*. New York. v. 9, no. 9 (August 1947), p. [1]-40.
(Abridged Edition) Not seen. "Abridged from the books in the author's own words." Issued in illustrated wrappers. Original price unknown. The current price range is estimated at between $15 and $30. Copies of this edition are very scarce. *References:* NUC, Bantam.

f. *The New York Post*, 1947. ?p.
(Condensed Edition) Not seen. Published in October of 1947. Original price unknown. The current price range is estimated at between $30 and $50. Copies of this version are very scarce. *Reference:* Bantam.

g. London: William Heinemann Ltd., [1947]. 254p.
(First British Edition) Not seen. Published in November of 1947. Bound in coarse red cloth. Lettering and ornaments on the spine are stamped in silver. The Heinemann windmill is blind-stamped on the lower right-hand corner of the back cover. All of the edges are unstained and trimmed. Issued with buff end papers. Issued in a green dust jacket printed in white and black. Two variant bindings have been noted. The first is in purple cloth. The second is in blue cloth with the front cover printed in black with a circular ex libris device. Lettering and rules on the spine are printed in black. This latter variant lacks the half title page and the page containing the list of books by the same author. Originally priced at 9s. 6d., with a current price range estimated at between $25 and $45. Copies of this edition are very scarce. *References:* GP-A23b, BM-183, NUC, CBI, EC.

h. New York: Grosset & Dunlap, 1948. 312p.
(Reprint Edition) Not seen. Published in February of 1948. Issued in a dust jacket with a new illustration by I. Docktop. Originally

priced at $1.49, with a current price range estimated at between $5 and $15. Copies of this edition are difficult to find. *References:* GP-A23f, BM-186, CBI.

i. [Roma]: The Albatross, [c1949]. ?p.
(The Modern Continental Library Edition) Not seen. Not to be introduced into the United States or Great Britain. Original price unknown. The current price range is estimated at between $35 and $75. Copies of this edition are scarce. *Reference:* GP-A23g.

j. New York: Bantam Books, [1950]. 246p.
(First Bantam Books Paperback Edition, No. 752) Not seen. Published in January of 1950. Originally priced at 25¢, with a current price range estimated at between $5 and $10. Copies of this edition are difficult to locate. *References:* GP-A23h, NUC, Bantam.

k. New York: The Viking Press, [1952?] ?p.
(Combined Edition) Not seen. Combined with *East of Eden*. There is some confusion with regard to this edition. Goldstone/Payne (A32g) give [c1953] as the date of publication and also state that this edition was a Book-of-the-Month Club selection. Yet in (A23i) they give [c1952] as the date of publication and do not mention the Book-of-the-Month Club at all. Since this has not been examined the answer to this mystery will have to await the discovery of more authoritative information. Original price unknown. The current price range is estimated at between $20 and $50. Copies of this edition are scarce. *Reference:* GP-A23i.

l. London: Transworld Publishers, [1953]. 246p.
(Corgi Books Paperback Edition, No. GN1374) Not seen. Published on November 24, 1952. Originally priced at 2s., with a current price range estimated at between $5 and $10. Copies of this edition are difficult to locate. *References:* GP-A23j, BNB, BBIP, EC.

m. New York: Grosset & Dunlap, [1957]. 312p.
(Second Grosset & Dunlap Reprint Edition) Not seen. Originally priced at $1.98, with a current price range estimated at between $5 and $15. Copies of this edition are difficult to find. *References:* CBI, BIP.

n. New York: Bantam Books, [1957]. 212p.
(New Bantam Books Paperback Edition, No. A1555) Not seen.

Originally priced at 35¢, with a current price range estimated at between $5 and $10. Copies of this edition are hard to find. *References:* BIP, Bantam.

o. London: Heinemann, [1967]. 254p.
(A Reissue of the 1947 Edition) Not seen. Published on May 1, 1967. Originally priced at 30s., with a current price range estimated at between $10 and $20. Copies of this edition are difficult to find. *References:* GP-A23k, BNB, EC, BBIP, CBI, NUC.

p. New York: Doubleday Dollar Book Club, 1967. ?p.
(Subscription Edition) Not seen. Published in May of 1967. Original price unknown. The current price range is estimated at between $15 and $35. Copies of this edition are scarce. *References:* GP-A23l, Bantam.

q. [London]: Distributed by Heron Books, [1971]. 253p.
(Heron Uniform Edition) Issued in the Heron uniform imitation leather binding. Original illustrations are by Bruce Drysdale. Original price unknown. The current price range is estimated at between $100 and $200. Copies of this edition are very scarce. *References:* GP-A23n, CBI, NUC, SRC.

r. [Harmondsworth, Eng.; New York]: Penguin Books, 1979. 212p.
(First Penguin Paperback Edition) Carries a new cover design by Neil Stuart. Originally priced at $2.95, and 95s., with a current price range estimated at between $5 and $10. Copies of this edition are fairly common. *References:* NUC, CBI.

62. *The Winter of Our Discontent* (1961)

a. New York: The Viking Press, 1961. 311p.
(First Edition, Limited Issue) Published in April of 1961 in a limited edition of 500 copies specially printed and bound for friends of the author and publishers. Page [i] contains the limitation notice. Bound in dark blue buckram with bevelled edges. The front cover is stamped in gold with John Steinbeck's signature. Lettering and rules on the spine are also stamped in gold. The top edges are stained yellow and all of the edges are trimmed. Has yellow end papers. Issued in a blue pictorial dust jacket designed by Elmer Hader with lettering by Jeanyee Wong. Also has a clear cellophane over jacket stamped in red: LIMITED EDITION. Not for sale. The

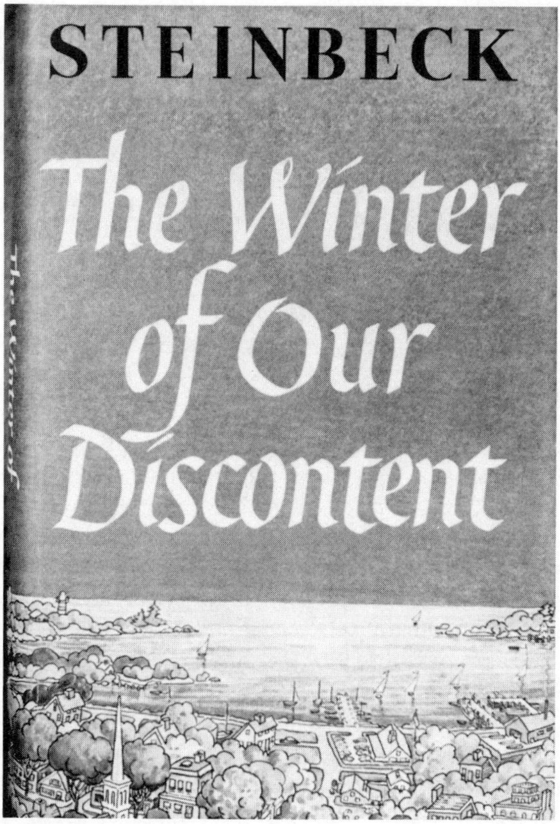

First edition limited issue of "The Winter of Our Discontent," with dust jacket designed by Elmer Hader and lettering by Jeanyee Wong.

current price range is estimated at between $150 and $250. Copies of this limited issue of the first edition are very scarce. *References:* GP-A38a, BM-251, NUC, SRC.

b. New York: The Viking Press, 1961. 311p.
(First Edition, Regular Trade Issue) Also published in April of 1961. The limitation notice is omitted from page [i]. Bound in bright blue cloth. The front cover is stamped in blind with a Viking ship. The spine is stamped in silver vertically from top to bottom: JOHN/ *[horizontally on a black background in silver] [double rule]*/ THE/ WINTER/ OF OUR/ DIS-/ CONTENT/ *[double*

rule] [vertically from top to bottom] STEINBECK. The top edges are stained blue, and all of the edges are trimmed. Issued in the same colored pictorial dust jacket as the first edition, limited issue. Originally priced at $4.50, with a current price range estimated at between $35 and $75. Copies of this edition are relatively easy to find. *References:* GP-A38b, BM-252, NUC, CBI, SRC.

c. Toronto: Macmillan, 1961. 311p.
(First Canadian Edition) Not seen. Published at the same time as the Viking Press edition. Originally priced at $4.95, with a price range estimated at between $15 and $40. Copies of this edition are difficult to find. *References:* GP-A38d, CBI.

d. London: William Heinemann Ltd., 1961. 365p.
(First British Edition) Published on June 26, 1961. Bound in purple cloth. Lettering on the spine is stamped in gold. The Heinemann windmill is blind-stamped on the lower right-hand corner of the back cover. All of the edges are unstained and trimmed. Issued in a rose decoration, pictorial dust jacket printed in yellow and white, designed by Lacey Everett. Originally priced at 18s., with a current price range estimated at between $15 and $35. Copies of this edition are scarce. *References:* GP-A38c, BM-254, NUC, BNB, EC, CBI, SRC.

e. Pleasantville, N.Y.: Reader's Digest Association, [1961]. 574p.
(Reader's Digest Condensed Books Edition) Published in July of 1961 in condensed form along with several other works. Illustrations for this condensation are by Steven Dohanos. Issued in a dust jacket with the publisher's oversize wraparound band. There appears to be several variants of this edition all of which cannot be identified at this writing. Original price unknown. The current price range is estimated at between $25 and $50. Copies of this edition are fairly common especially without a dust jacket. *References:* BM-257, Bantam, BRL.

f. New York: The Viking Press, 1961. ?p.
(Literary Guild Edition) Published in August of 1961. Bound in blue cloth covers with gray spine. The top edges stained yellow. There is no indication of Book Club edition on the dust jacket. Original price unknown. The current price range is estimated at between $25 and $50. Copies of this edition are scarce. *References:* GP-A38f, Bantam, SRC.

g. New York: The Viking Press, 1961. 281p.
(Book-of-the-Month Club Edition) Bound in gray cloth. The top edges are stained yellow. The statement "Book Club Selection" is included on the front inner fold of the dust jacket. Two thicknesses of paper have been noted: 22 mm. and 20 mm. thick. Bantam books indicate that the Book-of-the-Month Club alternate selection was issued in September of 1962. Original price unknown. The current price range is estimated at between $15 and $30. Copies of this edition are fairly common. *References:* GP-A38e, BRL.

h. Louisville, Ky.: American Printing House for the Blind, [c1961]. 3v.
(Braille Edition) Not seen. Original price unknown. No price range or availability determined. *Reference:* GP-A38g.

i. [Taipei, Taiwan: no publisher indicated, 1961]. 311p.
(Pirated Edition) Not seen. This edition is printed on rice paper and the title paper is altered from the first edition sheets. Bound in moss green cloth and the lettering on the spine is stamped in silver. Issued in a white coated paper dust jacket printed in red, reproducing in monochrome the original Elmer Hader dust jacket. A variant red cloth binding has been noted. Original price unknown. The current price range is estimated at between $25 and $55. Copies of this edition are rare. *References:* GP-A38i, BM-256, NUC, MB-95.

j. New York: Bantam Books, [1962]. 298p.
(First Bantam Books Paperback Edition, No. S2461). Published in November of 1962. All of the edges are stained yellow and trimmed. Originally priced at 75¢, with a current price range estimated at between $5 and $10. Copies of this edition are still fairly common. *References:* GP-A38h, NUC, BIP, SRC, BRL.

k. London: Pan Books, [1963]. 282p.
(First Pan Books Paperback Edition, No. M38) Published on July 5, 1963. Later printings have been noted. Originally priced at 5s., with a current price range estimated at between $5 and $10. Copies of this edition are difficult to locate. *References:* GP-38j, BBIP, WCBL, BRL (1977 printing).

l. [London]: Distributed by Heron Books, [1971]. 366p.
(Heron Uniform Edition) Issued in the uniform imitation leather binding. Original illustrations are by Virginia Smith. Original price

unknown. The current price range is estimated at between $100 and $200. Copies of this edition are very difficult to find. *References:* GP-A38k, BM-258, NUC, CBI, SRC.

m. New York: The Viking Press, [c1973]. 311p.
(Apparently a Reprint Edition) Not seen. Two variant bindings have been noted. One is bound in brown cloth stamped in silver and red. The top edges are unstained and it has brown end papers. The other is bound in half imitation brown leather on the spine which is stamped in silver and blue. The covers are bound in mustard-colored imitation leather. Apparently issued without a dust jacket. Original price unknown. The current price range is estimated at between $10 and $20. Copies of this edition are very difficult to find. *References:* BM-259 & 260.

n. [Harmondsworth, Eng.; New York]: Penguin Books, [1982]. 324p.
(First Penguin Books Paperback Edition) Not seen. Carries a new cover design by Neil Stuart. Orginally priced at $3.95, with a current price range estimated at between $5 and $10. Copies of this edition are still in print and quite common. *References:* BIP, CBI.

o. [Harmondsworth, Eng.; New York]: Penguin Books, [1983]. 311p.
(Reprint Television Edition) Bound in blue wrappers with photographs on the front cover of Donald Sutherland, Teri Garr, and Tuesday Weld who starred in the CBS Television Hallmark Hall of Fame presentation in December of 1983. The cover design is by Donna DeCesare. Originally priced at $3.95. No price range because this edition is still in print. *References:* BIP, BRL.

5. Chronological Checklist of Steinbeck's Major Works

It will be useful to the collector of Steinbeck collectible editions to see his major works placed in the order of their appearance in print. A chronological listing provides a sense of relationship, which is important in determining book values.

The checklist below includes only the first editions of each title. Each citation includes full bibliographical information. Where there is more than one title published in a year, they have been placed in chronological order. Whenever the exact publication date is unknown, the titles have been placed at the end of each yearly segment.

1929

Steinbeck, John. *Cup of Gold, A Life of Henry Morgan, Buccaneer, with Occasional Reference to History*. New York: Robert M. McBride & Company, 1929. 269p.

1932

________. *The Pastures of Heaven*. New York: Brewer, Warren & Putnam, 1932. 294p.

1933

________. *To a God Unknown*. New York: Robert O. Ballou, [1933]. 325p.

1935

________. *Tortilla Flat*. Illustrated by Ruth Gannett. New York: Covici-Friede Publishers, [1935]. 316p.

1936

________. *In Dubious Battle*. New York: Covici-Friede Publishers, [1936]. 349p.

________. *Nothing So Monstrous, A Story*. [New York: The Pynson Printers, 1936]. 30p.

________. *Saint Katy the Virgin*. [New York: Covici-Friede Publishers, 1936]. 25 [1]p.

1937

________. *Of Mice and Men*. New York: Covici-Friede Publishers, [1937]. 186p.

________. *The Red Pony*. New York: Covici-Friede Publishers, 1937. 81p.

________. *Of Mice and Men: Play*. New York: Covici-Friede Publishers, [1937]. 172p.

Kirkland, Jack. *Tortilla Flat, A Play in Three Acts*. Based on the novel by John Steinbeck and dramatized by Jack Kirkland. New York: Covici-Friede Publishers, [1937]. ?p.

1938

Steinbeck, John. *Their Blood Is Strong*. San Francisco: Simon J. Lubin Society of California, Inc., 1938. 33p.

________. *The Long Valley*. New York: The Viking Press, 1938. 303p.

1939

________. *The Grapes of Wrath*. New York: The Viking Press, [1939]. 619p.

1940

________. *John Steinbeck Replies*. [New York: Friends of Democracy, Inc., 1940]. [4]p.

1941

________. *The Forgotten Village*. New York: The Viking Press, 1940. 143p.

________. *Sea of Cortez, A Leisurely Journal of Travel and Research with a Scientific Appendix Comprising Material for a Source Book on the Marine Animals of the Panamic Faunal Provence*. With Edward F. Ricketts. New York: The Viking Press, 1941. 598p.

1942

________. *The Moon Is Down, a Novel*. New York: The Viking Press, 1942. 188p.

________. *The Moon Is Down, Play in Two Parts*. [New York]: Dramatists Play Service, Inc., [1942]. 101p.

_______. *Bombs Away, The Story of a Bomber Team*. New York: The Viking Press, 1942. 185p.

1943

_______. *The Viking Portable Library Steinbeck*. Selected by Pascal Covici. New York: The Viking Press, [1943]. 568p.

_______. *How Edith McGillcuddy Met R L S*. Cleveland: The Rowfant Club, 1943. 18p.

_______. *The Steinbeck Pocket Book*. Philadelphia: The Blakiston Company; distributed by Pocket Books Inc., New York, [1943]. 308p.

1945

_______. *Cannery Row*. New York: The Viking Press, 1945. 208p.

1947

_______. *The Wayward Bus*. New York: The Viking Press, 1947. 312p.

_______. *Vanderbilt Clinic*. [New York: The Presbyterian Hospital, 1947]. [13]p.

_______. *The Pearl*. With drawings by José Clemente Orozco. New York: The Viking Press, 1947. 122p.

_______. *The First Watch*. [Los Angeles, Calif.: The Ward Ritchie Press], Christmas, 1947. 6p.

1948

_______. *A Russian Journal*. With pictures by Robert Capa. New York: The Viking Press, 1948. 220p.

_______. *Foreword to* "Between Pacific Tides." [Stanford, Calif.: Privately Printed], 1948. [viii]p.

1950

_______. *Burning Bright, A Play in Story Form*. New York: The Viking Press, 1950. 159p.

1951

_______. *Burning Bright, A Play in Three Acts*. [New York]: Dramatists Play Service, [1951]. 56p.

_______. *The Log from the Sea of Cortez, The Narrative Portion of the Book, Sea of Cortez*. New York: The Viking Press, 1951. 282p. (Here reissued with a profile "About Ed Ricketts" by John Steinbeck.)

1952

________. *East of Eden*. New York: The Viking Press, 1952. 602p.

________. *Chapter Thirty-Four from the Novel East of Eden*. [Bronxville, N.Y.: Privately Printed, 1952]. [12]p.

McMahon, Luella E. *The Leader of the People, A Play in One Act*. Dramatized by Luella E. McMahon from a story by John Steinbeck. Chicago: Dramatic Publishing Company, [1952]. 27p.

1953

Steinbeck, John. *The Short Novels of John Steinbeck*. New York: The Viking Press, 1953. 407p.

________. *Viva Zapata!* [Roma: Babuina; Dist. Ediaioni Dell'atoneo, 1953]. 182p.

1954

________. *Sweet Thursday*. New York: The Viking Press, 1954. 273p.

1955?

________. *Positano*. Salerno: Ente Provinciale per Ilturismo, [1955?]. 30p.

1956

Rodgers, Richard. *Pipe Dream*. Book and Lyrics by Oscar Hammerstein II. Based on *Sweet Thursday* by John Steinbeck. New York: The Viking Press, 1956. 158p.

Steinbeck, John. *Un Américain à New-York et à Paris*. Paris: René Julliard, [1956]. 154p.

1957

________. *The Short Reign of Pippin IV, a Fabrication*. New York: The Viking Press, 1957. 188p.

1958

________. *Once There Was a War*. New York: The Viking Press, 1958. 233p.

1961

________. *The Winter of Our Discontent*. New York: The Viking Press, 1961. 311p.

Lawrence, Reginald. *Molly Morgan, A Play in Three Acts*. Chicago: Dramatic Publishing Company, [1961]. 104p. (Dramatized by Reginald Lawrence from a story by John Steinbeck from *The Pastures of Heaven*.)

1962

Steinbeck, John. *Travels with Charley: In Search of America*. New York: The Viking Press, [1962]. 246p.

________. *Speech Accepting the Nobel Prize for Literature*. New York: The Viking Press, [1962 or 3]. 10 [1]p.

1964

________. *A Letter from John Steinbeck Explaining Why He Could Not Write an Introduction for this Book*. [New York: Random House, 1964]. 7p.

________. *A Letter from John Steinbeck*. [Aptos, California]: Roxburghe & Zamorano Clubs, 1964. [12]p.

1966

________. *America and Americans*. New York: The Viking Press, [1966]. 207p.

1969

________. *Journal of a Novel: the East of Eden Letters*. New York: The Viking Press, [1969]. 182p.

1970

________. *John Steinbeck: His Language*. Aptos, California: [Roxburghe & Zamorano Clubs], 1970. [14]p.

1975

________. *Steinbeck: A Life in Letters*. Edited by Elaine Steinbeck and Robert Wallsten. New York: The Viking Press, [1975]. 906p.

Frost, Warren Lindsay. *John Steinbeck's The Pearl*. Dramatized by Warren Frost. Chicago: The Dramatic Publishing Company, [1975]. 76p.

1976

Malory, Sir Thomas. *The Acts of King Arthur and His Noble Knights*. [By] John Steinbeck: from [Malory's] Winchester mss. and other sources. Edited by Chase Horton. New York: Farrar, Straus and Giroux, [1976]. 363p.

1978

Steinbeck, John. *Letters to Elizabeth: A Selection of Letters from John Steinbeck to Elizabeth Otis*. San Francisco, Calif.: Book Club of California, 1978. 119p.

III. Information Sources

Appendix A: Directory of Booksellers

Buying by mail is perhaps the most important or possibly the only way we have to purchase the Steinbeck materials for our various collections. It is also a good way to learn about prices and the material itself. Most booksellers offer catalogs from which you can choose the items you want. Because of the high costs involved in producing printed catalogs, you may have to pay a small sum to receive them on a regular basis. In the long run this expense is well worth it given the amount of useful information many of these catalogs contain.

Below is a selected list of twenty antiquarian booksellers who have offered Steinbeck materials in the past or who tend to specialize in his works or those about him.

Argosy Book Store, Inc.
116 East 59th Street
New York, N.Y. 10022
(212) 753-4455

General antiquarian bookseller specializing in literature. Issues periodic catalogs. Prices tend to run on the high side.

Argus Books & Graphics
1714 Capitol Avenue
Sacramento, California 95814
(916) 443-2223

General antiquarian bookseller. No catalogs noted. A visit to this bookseller revealed that Steinbeck prices were reasonable.

Steven C. Bernard
First Editions
138 New Mark Esplanade

Rockville, Maryland 20850
(301) 340-8623

General antiquarian bookseller specializing in literature. Issues periodic catalogs. Prices tend to be in the medium range.

Preston C. Beyer
Fine Literary Property
752A Pontiac Lane
Oronoque Village
Stratford, Connecticut 06497
(203) 375-9073

Mr. Beyer is one of the cofounders of the John Steinbeck Society of America and an experienced Steinbeck expert. Issues regular catalogs which usually contain many Steinbeck collectible editions at reasonable prices.

The Book Nest
366 Second Street
Los Altos, California 94022
(415) 948-4724

Ed Schmitz of the Book Nest specializes in all phases of Steinbeck collectible materials. This author has seen no catalogs, but a visit to his store reveals that his prices are reasonable.

Danville Books
176 South Hartz Avenue
Danville, California 94526
(415) 837-4200

General bookseller with special interests in Steinbeckiana. This author has seen no catalogs.

James M. Dourgarian – Bookman
179 Saranap Avenue
Walnut Creek, California 94595-1156
(415) 935-5033

Mr. Dourgarian is a Steinbeck specialist and collector as well as a general antiquarian bookseller. Issues catalogs from time to time. Tends to have very reasonable prices.

Heritage Bookshop, Inc.
847 North La Cienega Blvd.
Los Angeles, California 90069
(213) 659-3674

General antiquarian bookseller with a specialty in Californiana. Issues occasional catalogs. Prices tend to be on the high side.

John Howell—Books
434 Post Street
San Francisco, California 94102
(415) 781-7795

General antiquarian bookseller specializing in rare books, prints and manuscripts. Occasionally issues catalogs. Prices tend to be in the high range.

Kenneth Karmiole Booksellers, Inc.
2255 Westwood Blvd.
Los Angeles, California 90064
(213) 474-7305

General antiquarian bookseller. Issues occasional catalogs. Prices tend to be in the medium range.

J. Stephan Lawrence Rare Books
230 North Michigan Avenue, Suite 205
Chicago, Illinois 60601

General antiquarian bookseller. Issues periodic catalogs in various fields including literature. Prices tend to be in the medium range.

Mitchell Books
1635 North Michigan Avenue
Pasadena, California 91104

John Mitchell is a Steinbeck specialist and issues occasional catalogs. His prices generally fall in the medium range.

Bradford Morrow Bookseller Ltd.
33 West 9th Street
New York, N.Y. 10011
(212) 477-1136

General antiquarian bookseller with a sideline in Steinbeck materials. Issues periodic catalogs. Prices tend to be in the high range.

Maurice F. Neville Rare Books
835 Laguna Street
Santa Barbara, California 93101
(805) 963-1908

General antiquarian bookseller. Has a fair sampling of Steinbeck materials. Issues catalogs. Prices tend to be on the high side.

Sal Noto – Bookscout
21995 McClellan Road
Cupertino, California 95014
(408) 253-7864

Apparently specializes in books by major authors including John Steinbeck. No catalogs noted.

C.R. Perryman – Books
P.O. Box 333
Temple, Georgia 30179
(404) 562-3084

General bookseller with a particular specialty in Steinbeck's Periodical appearances. This author has not seen any catalogs.

Diane Peterson – Booklady
P.O. Box 2544
Atherton, California 94025
(415) 324-1201

General bookseller with a particular interest in John Steinbeck. Prices usually fall in the middle range. Issues periodic catalogs.

Randall and Windle
185 Post Road
San Francisco, California 94108
(415) 781-2218

General antiquarian bookseller specializing mostly in rare books. Issues periodic catalogs. Prices tend to be quite reasonable.

Serendipity Books, Inc.
1790 Shattuck Avenue
Berkeley, California 94709
(415) 841-7455

General antiquarian bookseller who handles author collections. Issues occasional catalogs. Prices tend to be in the medium range.

William P. Wreden, Books & Manuscripts
200 Hamilton Avenue
P.O. Box 56
Palo Alto, California 94302
(415) 325-6851

General antiquarian bookseller. No catalogs noted.

Appendix B: The Language of Collecting

Every specialized profession or activity creates its own jargon, much of which is unintelligible to the layperson. Book collecting is no exception. Over the centuries since the invention of the printing press and the printed book, a terminology has developed uniquely related to the distribution and collection of printed materials.

As a collector of Steinbeck editions, you will find it helpful to become acquainted with abbreviations and terms employed by booksellers in their catalogs and transactions. The objective of this section is to isolate and define such abbreviations, words and phrases commonly used in book collecting that would be likely to confuse one faced for the first time by a bookseller's or auctioneer's catalog. The following lists are by no means exhaustive but do provide you with explanations of those you will most likely encounter in a search for Steinbeck materials.

Abbreviations

Booksellers' catalogs are by necessity filled with numerous abbreviations, and most assume a basic knowledge of the meaning of these abbreviations without offering an explanation. Take for example the following:

> 184. Steinbeck, John
> In Dubious Battle...New York: Covici-Friede, [1936].
> First trade edition. 12 mo. 349pp. Yellow cloth with a small ink stain on the back cover. A good copy in a dj that has a few small chips on the lower spine.

The following abbreviations are those found to occur most frequently in booksellers' catalogs.

ABAA—Antiquarian Booksellers' Association of America, Incorporated
ABPC—*American Book Prices Current*
abr—abridged
ACs—autographed card
ad, adv—advertisement
ADs—autograph document, signed
a.e.g.—all edges gilt
a.l.s.—autograph letter, signed
AMs s—autograph manuscript, signed
anon—anonymous
anr—another
ANs—autograph note, signed
b—born
BAL—*Bibliography of American Literature*
BAR—*Book Auction Records*
bd—bound
bdg—binding
bds—boards
bf—boldface (type)
bib—bibliography
bkrm—buckram
bkstrp—backstrip
BPC—*Book Prices Current*
BPI—*Bookman's Price Index*
bxd—boxed
c—copyright, or circa
ca—circa
cat—catalog
cf—calf
chpd—chipped
cl—cloth
coa—cash on arrival
cod—cash on delivery
col—color
comp—compiled
cond—condition
cont—contemporary
cor—cash on receipt
cwo—cash with order

dec – decorated
dj – dust jacket
ds – document, signed
dup – duplicate
dw – dust wrapper (same as dust jacket)
ed – edition, editor
edn – edition
eng – engraved, engraving
ep – end paper
ex – example
ex-ill – extra-illustrated
ex-lib – ex-library copy
f or F – folio
f – fine condition
facs – facsimile
first – first edition
f/l – fly leaf
fldg – folding
fol – folio size
front(is) – frontispiece
fx – foxed or foxing
g – good condition
g.e. – gilt edges
g.l. – gothic letter
gt. – gilt
g.t. – gilt top
hf bd – half bound in leather
hf cf – half bound in calf
h.t.v.b. – hors texte, versos blank (outside of the text, left-hand pages are blank)
illus – illustrated or illustrations
impft. – imperfect
inscr – inscribed
l or ll – leaf or leaves
lea – leather
lev – levant
lg or lge – large
litho – lithographed
l.p. – large paper
l.s. – letter, signed
ltd – limited
ltd. edn – limited edition
m.e. – marbled edges

mor—morocco
ms—manuscript
mtd—mounted
n.d.—no date
no.—number
n.p.—no place
n.y.—no year
ob—oblong
o.p.—out of print
orig—original
o.s.—out of stock
o/w—otherwise
p.—page (also pp. for pages)
pict—pictorial
pl(s).—plate(s)
port—portrait
p.p.—post paid or privately printed
prelims—preliminary leaves
pref—preface
pres—presentation copy
pseud—pseudonym
pt.—part
ptd—printed
pub—publisher, published, publication
rev—revised
SASE—self-addressed stamped envelope
ser.—series
sgd—signed
sig—signature
sm—small
spec bdg—special binding
spr—sprinkled
stns—stains
swd.—sewed
t.e.g.—top edge gilt
thk—thick
t.l.s.—typed letter, signed
t.p.—title page
transl.—translated
unbd—unbound
v.d.—various dates
v.g.—very good condition
vol—volume

v.p. – various places
w.a.f. – with all faults
wrps – wrappers
y.e. – yellow pages

Terminology

The terms used in book collecting are reasonably standardized. At the same time they, like abbreviations, have special uses restricted to this field. The following is a list of terms and definitions commonly used among dealers and collectors of modern antiquarian books.

Addenda – material added to the end of a book, usually to correct published errors or furnish omitted material.

All edges gilt (a.e.g.) – outer edges of leaves of book cut smooth and gilded with gold leaf.

Anonymous – a book published without an author's name given.

Association copy – a book once owned by someone associated with the author of a particular work, or by the author.

Authorized edition – a legitimate or nonpirated edition.

Autograph copy – a book signed by the author.

Backstrip – the spine of a book.

Binding – the exterior covering of a book.

Binding copy – a book in such a poor state that it is fit only for rebinding.

Blank leaves – usually at the beginning or end of a book, and noted in collation of a work, since they represent an integral part of the book.

Blind stamp – an impression made in the paper, or binding, often to indicate ownership.

Boards – stiff cardboard material used for the covers of a book. This is usually covered with cloth or leather. However, when cardboard material is covered with paper or left uncovered, the resultant book is said to be "in boards." Pictorial boards refer to those with illustrations.

Book plate—consists of a printed label which, when affixed to the inside cover or fly leaf of a book, indicates ownership. These may be important in establishing a book as an association copy.

Book sizes—A method of classifying books according to format devised during the fifteenth century. Printers would fold large printed sheets, and the resulting book was classified according to the number of folds used. For example, one fold constitutes a folio (two leaves), two folds a quarto (four leaves), three folds an octavo (eight leaves), and so on. However, unless the size of the original sheet is known, confusion may arise. Contemporary books, though still described according to the classic terminology, are classified more in terms of their actual physical dimensions. The table below may be used as a guide to this classification. A book should be placed in that classification to which its dimensions most nearly correspond:

Elephant Folio	23″ or taller
F (folio)	13″ or taller
4to (quarto)	12″
8vo (Octavo)	9″
12mo (duodecimo)	7–8″
16mo (sextodecimo)	6–7″
24mo (vigesimoquarto)	5–6″
32mo (trigesimosecundo)	4–5″
48mo (fortyeightmo)	4″ or less
64mo (sixtyfourmo)	3″
Miniature	under 3″ tall

As a general rule most paperbacks are 16mo, novels 12mo or 8vo, and non-fiction 8vo or sometimes 4to. Uncommonly sized books and rare books should be described with exact measurements.

Broadside—a posterlike sheet of paper printed on one side only and used mostly for announcements or advertisements.

Buckram—a coarse or heavy fabric made from linen or cotton and used for bookbinding. Longer-lasting than ordinary cloth binding material and thus often used for library books.

Bumped—refers to areas of wear on the binding of a book: e.g., "spine bumped," "covers bumped," etc.

Calf—a leather binding made from calfskin or sheepskin. If not specially treated it tends to deteriorate with age.

Cancel—leaf or slip of paper pasted over or tipped in to cancel or indicate printed errors.

Case—the cover of a book.

Chipped or **chipping**—refers to small nicks or marring on a book cover. This can also represent small pieces missing from a spine or dust jacket.

Cloth boards—refers to boards covered with cloth.

Collation—a careful examination of the physical format of a book in order to check for complete contents in proper order. All fly leaves, printed pages, plates, maps, etc. must be in proper sequence as recorded by bibliographers.

Colophon—commonly refers to an inscription on the last page of a book which gives the name of the publisher or printer and the date and place of publication; it may sometimes contain other information as well. Some colophons take the form of an emblem or symbol. Because modern-day books use title or copyright pages to supply publishing information, colophons are quite uncommon today.

Color plates—consist of colored illustrations included in a book. Many times color plates become the chief value of a book.

Condition—physical state of a book related to wear. May have a great effect on the value of a book regardless of its rarity.

Conjugate leaves—refers to leaves connected to each other to form a single piece of paper.

Contemporary binding—a binding in the style of the period during which a book was published, though not necessarily the original binding.

Copyright page—the back or verso of the title page of a book. Contains copyright data and many times other publishing information. Sometimes information on this page is the only way in which specific editions can be identified.

Corners—top and bottom tips of a book cover. Sometimes specially protected with leather or other material.

Covers bound in—a method by which a deteriorated and damaged original binding is saved when a book is rebound. Usually the original is included at the end of the book and may help prove its authenticity.

Cut—an illustration from an engraving. For example, a woodcut is a print made from an engraving on wood.

Deckle edge—untrimmed, rough edges of a leaf, often present in handmade paper but occasionally simulated by machine.

Dedication copy—a book inscribed by the author to the person to whom it is dedicated.

Dentelle—lacework patterns appearing on a book binding, especially around the edges of the covers.

Desiderata—lists of books wanted. Collectors and librarians present such lists to booksellers in order to acquire needed titles.

Device—a printer's mark or design.

Disbound—material without a binding.

Drop title—the title placed at the head of the first page of the text.

Dropped letter—indicates a missing printed letter.

Dust jacket or **Dust wrapper**—a protective paper cover, usually illustrated and/or printed, which is supplied by the publisher. These are often used as a means of advertising the book it covers or other books by the same publisher. A book that lacks its dust jacket often loses a substantial part of its value.

Edition—all the copies of a book printed from one setting of type.

End papers—lining paper, one half of which is pasted to the inside cover of the book (paste-down), the other half left free (free end paper). These may be plain, decorated or printed. Bookplates and inscriptions are frequently found on front end papers.

Ephemera—printed material of minor importance. Often of passing interest when first appearing. Includes posters, theatre programs, advertising circulars, railroad timetables, etc.

Errata—refers to errors in printing. Errata slips are used to note errors discovered after a book is printed but before it is released for distribution. These slips are normally pasted into the book.

Ex-library copy—a book discarded from a public, college, or lending library and bearing some kind of evidence of this such as a stamp, label, punch, etc. These are normally of less value in the book market.

Facsimile—an exact reproduction of a book. Generally produced by photo-offset and often difficult to distinguish from the original.

First edition—the first printing of a book. However, a first edition may have several "issues," the first usually being the most valuable. Issues come about due to some kind of alteration of the type during the printing of the first edition. Also an issue itself may have a separate "state," caused by a change in the book's binding, damaged type, inclusion of an errata slip and the like.

First separate edition—the first appearance of a work that previously appeared included with other material.

First trade edition—the first edition of a work that may have appeared initially in a limited edition or privately printed format.

Flyleaf—any blank leaf appearing between the free end paper and the first printed page at the beginning and end of a book.

Format—general appearance and makeup of a book including size, shape, paper, type, binding and overall arrangement.

Foxing—page discoloration in a book, usually brown or yellowish-brown. May be caused by impurities in the production of the paper or bacterial growth. Older books are commonly foxed and this does not necessarily affect their value. However, foxing should be noted when describing a book for sale.

Free end paper—the end paper that is not attached to the inside front cover.

Frontispiece—an illustration facing the title page of a book. Often the only illustration in a book and frequently a portrait of the author.

Galleys—the first set of proofs, usually printed on very long sheets of paper.

Gathering—a group of sheets folded together for sewing or gluing into the binding. Also called a signature.

Gilt edge—the application of gilt (gold leaf) to the edges of a book, usually the front and top edges.

Half-bound—a binding which uses one kind of material for the spine and another for the covers. The spine is usually leather-covered and the rest of the book either cloth or boards. Sometimes the cover tips may match the spine.

Half-title—a page appearing before the title page which contains only the title of the book (no subtitle or other information).

Headband—a fabric strip sewn or glued to the top and bottom (foot-band) edges of the spine of a book. Serves as a reinforcing agent or sometimes is purely decorative.

Hinge—the flexible interior area of a binding where the covers of a book and the backstrip join together. The exterior joining is more properly called the "joint," although in general usage the term "hinge" is used for both.

Holograph—any written material which is entirely in the author's handwriting.

Impression—one of a number of printings made at different times from the same set of type.

Imprint—name of publisher, usually indicating date and place of publication. Ordinarily appears at the bottom of the title page.

In print—copies of a book still available from the publisher.

Inscribed copy—a copy of a work specially autographed by the author for an individual whose name is mentioned in the inscription.

Inscription—a comment or phrase inscribed in a book, not necessarily by the author.

Inserted leaves—sheets tipped in after binding has been completed.

Integral—a leaf or page is said to be integral when it was sewn and bound into a book during the book's manufacture. The opposite of **Cancel**. (See **Cancel**)

Issue—a copy of the first edition of a book which somehow differs, either internally or externally, from other copies. (See also **First edition**)

Joint—See **Hinge**.

Labels—title and author of a book printed on paper, cloth or leather strips which are glued to the backstrip and/or cover of a book. Labels are used sparingly today.

Laid in—any material inserted into a book but not attached to it in any way. These items may include old letters, photographs, newspaper or magazine clippings and the like. In some instances the laid-in material may enhance the value of a book or be important on its own account: e.g., a letter written by the author.

Laid paper—usually handmade paper, with parallel lines watermarked in, and visible when the paper is held up to light.

Large-paper copy—a special book edition containing extra-wide margins. Usually produced with better grade paper and designed to appear more elegant.

Leaf—a single sheet in a book. Each leaf contains two printed pages, one on each side.

Levant—highly polished Moroccan leather.

Limited edition—a stated number of copies printed, anywhere from a few to several thousand, though normally under 4,000. Generally the copies are numbered consecutively and sometimes are signed by the author. Many limited edition books are quite valuable and in demand.

Limp—an adjective describing a flexible binding in suede or imitation leather such as that used on the early titles of the Modern Library. A paperback is not a limp binding.

Made-up or sophisticated copy—refers to an imperfect copy perfected by adding missing leaves or plates.

Marbled paper—book paper which is decorated with a veining-in-marble pattern.

Mint copy—a book in perfect condition.

Misbound—a book with a plate or gathering erroneously bound in.

Morocco—soft leather used for bookbinding and made from goatskin tanned with sumac. Originally from Morocco but now widely produced. (See also **Levant**)

No place (n.p.), **No date** (n.d.)—a bookseller's indication that no place and/or date of publication is noted within the book. However, if the place and/or date is known from another source, then this information may be noted in parentheses: e.g., No Place (Boston): No Date (1902).

Original cloth (boards, wrappers)—this indicates that the binding is as issued by the publisher.

Out of print—the material is no longer available from the publisher.

Part issues—a novel's first appearance in weekly or monthly parts issued in a magazine or separate wrappers.

Paste-down—the portion of the end paper pasted to the inner cover of a book.

Pictorial cloth—cloth bindings that contain pictures.

Pirated edition—any book or material issued or published without the consent of the author.

Point(s) – an identifying feature which distinguishes between different issues or states of an edition. Points are usually typographic in nature, such as misspelled words or incorrectly numbered pages and so on. However, a binding variation can also constitute a point. Point identification is a very complex and difficult process. The wise collector turns to the standard bibliography of a well-known author or subject in order to uncover all the points of an edition. The bibliography in hand is a good example.

Presentation copy – a book presented as a gift by the author to an individual, usually at the time of publication. Customarily contains a message and therefore becomes an inscribed copy as well.

Press books – refers to books issued from fine and private presses.

Printer's device – See **Device.**

Provenance – refers to the history of a book's ownership.

Pseudonym – an assumed name used for anonymity; a pen name: e.g., John Stern (John Steinbeck).

Rare – a book that is extremely scarce and usually not turned up by a specialist dealer more than once in ten years.

Reading copy – usually one that is more suitable for reading than collecting due to its poor condition.

Rebacked – the replacement of a worn-out backstrip or spine of a book.

Rebound – indicates that the original binding has been completely replaced.

Recased – a book removed from and then replaced in its covers to preserve its condition after it has become loosened. Glue, resewing and sometimes new end papers are often involved when a book is recased.

Recto – the right-hand page of a book (odd numbered).

Remainder binding – unsold copies of a book sold en masse by the publisher to wholesalers or individual booksellers. Sometimes the new owner has the books rebound in a binding unlike the original.

Reprint – a new edition of a book; generally produced in a cheaper format but sometimes issued as a high-quality limited item.

Review copy – copy sent to a critic or reviewer, and sometimes constituting the earliest issue.

Rubbed – refers to the evidence of wear on a book's binding, but not yet badly worn.

Scarce – a hard-to-find book, usually not seen by a specialist bookseller more often than once a year.

Scuffed – indicates signs of wear on either a leather or cloth bound book. More severe than rubbing.

Shaken – loose between its covers.

Signature – a folded printed sheet in multiples of four that forms a section of a book. May contain four, eight, twelve, sixteen, or thirty-two pages to a section. Each individual signature is first sewn, then all signatures are gathered together for binding. Also known as a **gathering**. (See also **Book sizes**)

Signed copy – a book signed by the author and perhaps dated. Not the same as an "inscribed copy."

Slip case – a protective cardboard case covered with paper, cloth or leather into which a book is slipped when not in use. Often used in fine quality editions.

Spine – the back section of a binding which connects the front and back covers. The term "back" or "backbone" is commonly used to include both the spine and the backstrip which covers it.

Started – refers to the signature of a book that is loosening from a weak binding.

State – generally refers to a change other than a correction of a misprint. (See also **First edition**)

Sunned – Faded from exposure to light or direct sunlight. This usually occurs on spines (and can occur even through dust jackets), but it may happen to any exposed portion of a book. Green and purple are notoriously unstable colors, and books bound in those colors inevitably become sunned quickly.

Tail piece—an ornament which occupies a blank portion at the end of a page, chapter, section or the end of a book. Not the same as a "colophon."

Tipped in—any material attached with paste to a page or the binding of a book: e.g., a leaf, plate, errata slip. Not the same as "laid in."

Title page—in most cases located on the right-hand side at the beginning of a book, the title page contains the title, author or authors, publisher, date and place of publication. Sometimes part of this information may appear on the verso (or back, copyright page) of the title page.

Trimmed—having sheet edges that were roughly cut by the binder.

Uncut—a book whose leaf edges are untrimmed during the binding process. Not the same as "unopened," with which it is often confused.

Unopened—a book whose leaf edges have not been opened or cut apart. This is usually performed with a knife or letter opener. Paradoxically, an unopened (and therefore unread) book is considered more valuable to collectors than one that has been opened.

Unpaged—the pages are not numbered (although each signature may be designated by letter).

Variant—differentiation in text, color of cloth binding and so on, between copies of the same edition upon which rests no priority of issue.

Verso—a left-hand page of a book (even numbered). (See also **recto**)

Wove paper—usually machine-made, and distinguishable from laid paper in that no chain lines are visible when the paper is held up to light.

Waterstain—discoloration caused by water. Difficult to remove and best left to an expert.

Wrappers—a book trade term for stiff paper covers on a book or pamphlet. Today commonly known as a paperback publication.

Notes

Chapter 1

1. Preston C. Beyer, "John Steinbeck: The Forming of a Collection," *Steinbeck Quarterly* 12(Winter–Spring 1979): 32.

2. Ibid.

3. Lawrence Clark Powell, "On Collecting John Steinbeck," *The Book Collector's Packet* 12(July 1938): 11.

4. Victor Jones, *Creative Writing* (London: St. Paul's House, 1974), 17.

5. Paraphrased from a letter by Maurice Dunbar to the author, dated 30 November 1982.

6. Tetsumaro Hayashi, "Why Is Steinbeck's Literature Widely Read? – What Is the Essence of His Literature?" *Steinbeck Quarterly* 13(Winter–Spring 1980): 21.

7. Ibid.

8. Ibid.

9. Lee Richard Hayman, "Collecting Steinbeck: The Endless Hunt," *Steinbeck Quarterly* 12(Winter–Spring 1979): 48.

10. The classification scheme for types of Steinbeck materials discussed in this section was devised from one developed by Maurice Dunbar in an article entitled: "Collecting Steinbeck," *Steinbeck Quarterly* 12(Winter–Spring 1979): 42–48. I have expanded his original categories and appended my own comments plus additional examples where it seemed appropriate. This scheme is repeated in his new miniature book entitled *Steinbeck Collecting* (Venice, Fla.: Opuscula Press, 1983): 1–61.

Chapter 2

1. Allen Ahearn, *The Book of First Books*, 2nd ed. (Bethesda, Md.: Quill & Brush Press, 1978): 9.

2. Ibid., p. 6.

3. G.L. Brooks, *Books and Book-Collecting* (London: Andre Deutsch, 1980): 89.

4. Jack Matthews, *Collecting Rare Books for Pleasure and Profit* (New York: Putnam, 1977): 61. See also Arthur H. Minters, *Collecting Books for Fun and Profit* (New York: Arco, 1979): 49–50. Minters gives an excellent discussion of booksellers and the pricing process.

Chapter 3

1. Lee Richard Hayman, "Collecting Steinbeck: The Endless Hunt," *Steinbeck Quarterly* 12(Winter–Spring 1979): 49.

2. An excellent guide to organizing your collection is provided by Jean Peters in her article "Organizing a Collection" in *Book Collecting: A Modern Guide* (New York: Bowker, 1977): 159–182.

3. Hayman, *Ibid.*

4. Ronald E. Romano, *Collecting Old and Rare Books* (San Diego, Calif.: Kensington Press, 1979): 35.

5. An extensive discussion of auctions and how to use them for finding scarce items is contained in Robert A. Wilson's book *Modern Book Collecting* (New York: Knopf, 1980): 72–93.

6. Romano, *Ibid.*, p. 36.

7. The use of libraries by book collectors is well covered by Arthur H. Minters in his book *Collecting Books for Fun and Profit* (New York: Arco, 1979): 39–40. See also Hayman, *Ibid.*, and Romano, *Ibid.*, p. 39.

Chapter 4

1. Maurice Dunbar, *Books and Collectors* (Los Altos, Calif.: The Book Nest, 1980): 13.

2. Terry Belanger, "Descriptive Bibliography" in *Book Collecting: A Modern Guide*, edited by Jean Peters (New York: Bowker, 1977): 100.

3. William J. Henneman, "Bibliography of Books by John Steinbeck," *Reading and Collecting* 1(December 1936): 5, 18.

4. Lawrence Clark Powell, "Toward a Bibliography of John Steinbeck," *The Colophon* (New series) 3(Autumn 1938): 558–568.

5. Harry Thornton Moore, *The Novels of John Steinbeck: A First Critical Study* (Chicago: Normandie House, 1939): 97–101.

7. Tetsumaro Hayashi, *John Steinbeck: A Concise Bibliography, 1930–65*, introduction by Warren G. French (Metuchen, N.J.: Scarecrow Press, 1967): 164p. Hayashi revised this work in 1973 with a new title: *A New Steinbeck Bibliography, 1929–1971*, also published by the Scarecrow Press, 225p. In 1983 a supplement was published covering the years 1971–1981, 147p. This supplement carries an introduction by Robert DeMott.

8. Adrian Goldstone and John R. Payne, *John Steinbeck: A Bibliographical Catalogue of the Adrian H. Goldstone Collection* (Austin: Humanities Research Center, University of Texas at Austin, 1974).

9. Robert B. Harmon, *The First Editions of John Steinbeck* (Los Altos, Calif.: Hermes Publications, 1978): 14p.

10. Salinas Public Library, *John Steinbeck, A Guide to the Collection of the Salinas Public Library*, edited by John Gross and Lee Richard Hayman (Salinas, Calif.: The Salinas Public Library, 1979): 196p.

11. Bradford Morrow Bookseller, Ltd. [Catalogue Eight], *John Steinbeck: A Collection of Books and Manuscripts...* (Santa Barbara, Calif.: Bradford Morrow Bookseller, Ltd., 1980): 154p.

12. Stanford University Libraries, *A Catalogue of the John Steinbeck Collection at Stanford University*, compiled and edited by Susan F. Riggs (Stanford, Calif.: The Stanford University Libraries, 1980): 194p.

Annotated Bibliography

There are many secondary works, bibliographies of various kinds, directories, periodicals, general guides, and the like that are necessary aids to successful book collecting. We are extremely fortunate to have as many of these tools related to John Steinbeck as we do to assist us in our search for collectible editions of his works.

In compiling this book, for example, I found that in trade bibliographies such as *Books in Print* and *British Books in Print*, I was able to locate original prices of many Steinbeck editions not available elsewhere. National bibliographies like *The Cumulative Book Index* (CBI) and the *British National Bibliography* (BNB) were useful not only for price information but additional bibliographic detail as well. Fugitive Steinbeck editions were gleaned from the *British Museum Catalogue* and the *National Union Catalog* that are universal in scope. Then there are the bibliographies on Steinbeck himself, especially the ones compiled by Goldstone/Payne, Tetsumaro Hayashi, and the Salinas Pubic Library, which yielded much additional bibliographic information.

The list below, while extensive, is not exhaustive. There are other works in preparation that will be of benefit to book collectors. You can keep up-to-date on these by consulting the *Steinbeck Quarterly* or the *Steinbeck Collector*, discussed below.

A B Bookman's Weekly. Clifton, N.J.: A B Bookman Publications, Inc., 1948–.

A periodical devoted to listing books wanted and for sale. The bulk of each issue consists of dealers' advertisements for books wanted, with a smaller section of books for sale. The opening pages contain succinct reports of current news presented in a highly personal style with occasional articles by others. This publication is subscribed to not only by booksellers but also by collectors and librarians, who find it a pleasant and convenient way to keep in touch with current happenings. Address: P.O. Box AB, Clifton, New Jersey 07015.

Ahearn, Allen. *The Book of First Books*. 2d ed. Bethesda, Md.: Quill & Brush Press, 1978. 88p.

The introductory matter provides an excellent discussion of first editions, pricing structure, and what makes them collectible. The major portion lists first editions of famous authors, some "points," and current values.

American Book Prices Current. New York: American Book Prices Current, 1894/95–.

Generally considered the most accurate of the auction record compendia. Although arrangement and information given vary somewhat, information usually includes author, title, edition, place and date of publication, size, binding, condition, where sold, date of sale, catalog number of lot, and price.

Barker, David. *John Steinbeck: A Checklist*. [Salem, Oregon: David & Judy Barker, Booksellers, 1984]. 40p.

This checklist attempts to identify Steinbeck's major works published in the United States or Great Britain, including first trade editions, limited editions, advance and review copies, reprints and paperback editions, and the like. The list is arranged alphabetically by title, giving full bibliographical information and some brief descriptive data including suggested prices for various states or conditions. This checklist, although useful, is not comprehensive.

Belanger, Terry. "Descriptive Bibliography," In *Book Collecting: A Modern Guide*, ed. Jean Peters. New York: Bowker, 1977, 97–115. A concise but effective overview of descriptive bibliography. Emphasis is placed on the terms that a book collector must master before he or she can use descriptive bibliographies intelligently and read booksellers' catalogs wisely.

Beyer, Preston C. "John Steinbeck: The Forming of a Collection." *Steinbeck Quarterly* 12(Winter–Spring 1979): 32–42. Mr. Beyer, a prominent Steinbeck authority and bookseller, provides some insights into the world of Steinbeck collecting by sharing his experiences and offering helpful suggestions.

Bookman's Price Index. Detroit: Gale, 1964–. Basically a main entry list. The listings are based on descriptions of books and periodicals which were offered for sale by leading booksellers in their catalogs during the period covered. Includes a list of booksellers whose catalogs were scanned.

Books in Print. New York: Bowker, 1948– (annual). Commonly called BIP, this work lists current books alphabetically by author or title (separate volumes), with full bibliographic data on each book including price. There is also a separate subject index.

Boutell, Henry S. *First Editions of Today and How to Tell Them*. 4th ed. Berkeley, Calif.: Peacock Press, 1964.

A collection of statements from American and British publishers regarding the way first impressions are identified. This work should be used with caution.

Bradford Morrow Bookseller, Ltd. [Catalogue Eight] *John Steinbeck: A Collection of Books and Manuscripts...* Santa Barbara, Calif.: Bradford Morrow Bookseller, Ltd., 1980. 154p.

An illustrated bookseller's catalog of the Harry Valentine Collection. Lists some 700 items, including first editions, limited editions, periodicals, manuscripts, and the like. Has extensive and detailed notes on many items and a foreword by John R. Payne.

Bradley, Van Allen. *The Book Collector's Handbook of Values*. 4th ed. New York: Putnam, [1982]. 640p.

A useful handbook that includes an alphabetical author or anonymous title listing. The price range for copies in good condition is indicated, with a record of recent auction prices as applicable.

British Books in Print. London: J. Whitaker, 1874–.

Records books published in Great Britain in a dictionary arrangement by both author and title. Indicated publication information including prices. In 1971, it became a computer-produced annual with authors, titles, and catchwords in a single alphabetical sequence. The title varies.

British Museum, Dept. of Printed Books. *Catalogue of Printed Books*. London: The Trustees, etc., 1881–.

This is the catalog of Great Britain's major national library. Issued in a basic set with supplements every few years. Arranged by author or title entry. A good source for British editions of Steinbeck's works.

British National Bibliography. London: Council of the British National Bibliography, British Museum, 1950– (weekly).

An excellent national bibliography, arranged by Dewey Decimal classification. Includes classified subject section, author and title section, and subject index. Full bibliographic detail is provided, including prices.

Brook, George Leslie. *Books and Book-Collecting*. London: André Deutsch, 1980. 175p.

A general discussion of book collecting strategies and techniques written from a British perspective.

Carter, John. *A B C for Book Collectors*. 5th ed. London: Hart-Davis, Macgibbon, [1972]. 211p.

An authoritative alphabetical dictionary of bibliographic and booksellers' terms with definitions as used in Great Britain and the United States, sometimes giving examples based upon Carter's personal views and experiences.

Cumulative Book Index. New York: H.W. Wilson, 1898–.
Commonly called CBI, this publication represents a basic cumulative record of books published in the English language. Authors, titles, and subjects are in a single alphabetical arrangement, with the author entry giving complete bibliographical information including prices.

Dingman, Larry. *Bibliography of Limited and Signed Editions in Literature, Twentieth Century American Authors*. Stillwater, Minnesota: James Cummings Bookseller – Publisher, [1973]. 285p.
Designed as a guide for collectors, booksellers, librarians, and students of literary history whose special interests include the limited and signed editions of American literature. The books of each author are listed in chronological sequence and include only those hardcover books which were limited numerically or in small deluxe editions and were signed by the author at the time of publication. The listing of Steinbeck limited editions is on page 244 and is incomplete.

Directory of Specialized American Bookdealers. Prepared by the staff of the American Book Collector. New York: Moretus, [1984]. 344p.
Arranged by subject, with cross-references to booksellers contained in a separate alphabetical list along with addresses.

Dunbar, Maurice. *Books and Collectors*. Los Altos, Calif.: The Book Nest, 1980. 189p.
An excellent introductory work to the craft of book collecting. The novice will find this book helpful because of its readability. Dunbar offers many hints and suggestions on how to go about collecting books.

________. "Collecting Steinbeck." *Steinbeck Quarterly* 12(Winter–Spring 1979): 42–48.
The author creates a much-needed classification scheme for collection of Steinbeck materials. You will undoubtedly find this scheme very useful.

________. *Collecting Steinbeck*. Venice, Florida: Opuscula Press, 1983. 61p.
Dunbar enlarges upon his earlier classification scheme for Steinbeck collectibles in this miniature book.

English Catalogue of Books... London: S. Law, Publishers' Circular, 1801–1966 (ceased publication).
The standard English trade list during its period of publication. Frequency varied. Arrangement is alphabetical by author, with title and catchword subject entries in some volumes. Information given varies, but usually includes author, title, publisher, date, size, and price.

First Printings of American Authors: Contributions Toward Descriptive Checklists. Edited by Matthew J. Bruccoli and C.E. Frazer Clark, Jr. 4 vols. Detroit: Gale, 1977–1979.

Designed to provide basic bibliographic information on the first American and English printings of important writers. For each author there are three sections: principal works (including books and pamphlets), secondary works, and references. The individual entries provide the author's name and dates, and then they list, chronologically, books published. Each entry provides several reproduced title pages. Steinbeck is treated in Vol. 1, pp. 353-357.

Goldstone, Adrian H., and John R. Payne. *John Steinbeck: A Bibliographical Catalogue of the Adrian H. Goldstone Collection.* Austin: Humanities Research Center, University of Texas at Austin, 1974. 240p.

To date this work is the definitive descriptive bibliography on Steinbeck. Includes extensive bibliographic descriptions of major Steinbeck titles and lists many secondary and other source materials.

Haller, Margaret. *The Book Collector's Fact Book.* New York: Arco Publishing Co., Inc., 1976. 271p.

This work presents, in alphabetical order, facts about current book collecting practices, along with information on books as physical objects, and treats related topics. There is also information on the current status of the market on old books, and hints on how to check prices.

Harmon, Robert B. *The First Editions of John Steinbeck.* Los Altos, Calif.: Hermes Publications, 1978. 14p.

An extensive guide to first editions in a pocket-size format. Includes much descriptive bibliographic detail.

Hayashi, Tetsumaro. *John Steinbeck: A Concise Bibliography, 1930–65.* New York: Scarecrow Press, 1967. 164p.

The first major Steinbeck bibliography to be compiled and published. Useful for the collector in that it provides a classification scheme for Steinbeck materials.

________. *A New Steinbeck Bibliography, 1929–1971.* Metuchen, N.J.: Scarecrow Press, 1973. 225p.

A new revised and updated version of his 1967 bibliography.

________. *A New Steinbeck Bibliography: 1971–1981.* Metuchen, N.J: Scarecrow Press, 1983. 147p.

Essentially a supplement to his 1973 edition.

________. *A Handbook for Steinbeck Collectors.* (Steinbeck Monograph Series, No. 11) Muncie, Ind.: The Steinbeck Society of America, English Department, Ball State University, 1981. 54p.

A collection of previously published articles, mostly from the *Steinbeck Quarterly.* Includes materials relating to collecting Steinbeck items, evaluation of major collections, and articles on a prominent Steinbeck collector.

________. "Why Is Steinbeck's Literature Widely Read?—What Is the Essence of His Literature?" *Steinbeck Quarterly* 13(Winter-Spring 1980): 20–23.

Professor Hayashi details the basis of Steinbeck's popularity with the reading public both past and present. Along the way he provides some hints for collectors.

Hayman, Lee Richard. "Collecting Steinbeck: The Endless Hunt." *Steinbeck Quarterly* 12(Winter-Spring 1979): 48–53.

Mr. Hayman covers the many possible sources for finding Steinbeck materials and evaluates their productive value.

Henneman, William J. "Bibliography of Books by John Steinbeck." *Reading and Collecting* 1(December 1936): 5, 18.

A short descriptive bibliography of five Steinbeck titles published between 1929 and 1936. This was the first bibliography of a descriptive nature to be published on Steinbeck.

Iacone, Salvatore J. *The Pleasures of Book Collecting*. New York: Harper & Row, [1976]. 303p.

This work will appeal to a readership unacquainted with literature but anxious to invest in books. Basically a practical guide, this work is appropriate for beginners in the field.

International Book Collectors Directory. Vashon Island, Washington: Pegasus Press, 1983. 526p.

A sourcebook and "who's who and where" for book collectors, librarians, and booksellers. Lists book collectors, booksellers, and provides much other useful information.

Johnson, Merle DeVore. *Merle Johnson's American First Editions*. 4th ed., revised and enlarged by Jacob Blanck. New York: Bowker, 1942. 553p.

Lists the first editions of over 200 American authors of collectible interest. Gives important variants and collateral works.

McBride, William M. *A Pocket Guide to the Identification of First Editions*. 2d ed. Hartford, Conn.: The Author, 1982. 56p.

This guide discusses the methods that past and present English-language publishers use to identify their first editions of hardbound and paperback books. Issued in a pocket-size format.

________. *Points of Issue*. Hartford, Conn.: The Author, 1982. 76p.

This guide lists those major differences or "points" that identify the first or collectible editions of famous authors. Seven Steinbeck titles are listed on pages 65 and 66.

Matthews, Jack. *Collecting Rare Books for Pleasure and Profit*. New York: Putnam, 1977. 317p.

A discussion of rare books as investments, including first editions and so on. Also provides strategies and tactics in buying and selling.

Minters, Arthur H. *Collecting Books for Fun and Profit*. New York: Arco, 1979.

This work attempts to explain the methodology of selecting, ordering, paying for, cataloging, and caring for a collection of books. Generally Minters provides a good practical approach to book collecting.

Mitchell Books. [Catalog Six] *John Steinbeck*. [Pasadena, Calif.: Mitchell Books, 1982]. 68p.

An extensive bookseller's catalog devoted entirely to Steinbeck material. Lists some 204 items with detailed descriptive notes.

Moore, Harry Thornton. *The Novels of John Steinbeck: A First Critical Study*. Chicago: Normandie House, 1939. 102p.

Pages 97–101 contain a "Bibliographical Check-List of First Editions." This checklist includes nineteen items with descriptive information. Also included are several collections with Steinbeck contributions.

Patterson, R.H., ed. *Directory of American Book Specialists*. 3d. ed. New York: Continental, [1976]. 190p.

A general subject listing of booksellers and their specialties. One bookseller dealing in books by and about John Steinbeck is listed on page 175.

Peters, Jean, ed. *Book Collecting: A Modern Guide*. New York: Bowker, 1977. 288p.

A collection of twelve original essays that are practical, straightforward, up-to-date, and offers extensive references to other works. Collectors will find this book stimulating and informative.

_______, ed. *Collectible Books: Some New Paths*. New York: Bowker, 1979. 294p.

A collection of essays that discuss the importance of collecting nonfirst editions, book catalogs, mass market paperbacks and the like. Each essay is followed by a list of suggested further readings.

_______. "Organizing a Collection," in *Book Collecting: A Modern Guide*. Edited by Jean Peters. New York: Bowker, 1977. Pp. 159–182.

An excellent overview of how to organize your collection for easy access and how to keep track of materials. Provides helpful examples and illustrations.

Powell, Lawrence Clark. "John (Ernst) Steinbeck, 1902–." *Publishers' Weekly* 131(April 17, 1937): 1701.

A chronological list of Steinbeck's first seven major works including two additional items. Accompanying the bibliographical data are notes relating to publication information. This article was part of a series entitled "American First Editions" edited by Jacob Blanck.

_______. "On Collecting John Steinbeck." *The Book Collector's Packet* 12(July 1938): 11–12.

Powell comments on his early experiences as a Steinbeck enthusiast and collector. Along the way he provides some useful bibliographical information for Steinbeck collectors.

________. "Toward a Bibliography of John Steinbeck." *The Colophon* (New Series) 3(Autumn 1938): 558-568.

A predominantly bibliographical essay highlighting Powell's experiences in collecting Steinbeck first editions. Powell provides some valuable publication information not available elsewhere. At the conclusion is a "Check List of First Editions" up to 1938, arranged in chronological order with additional publication information. This article is very useful for those interested in the historical development of Steinbeck's early works.

Reference Catalogue of Current Literature... London: Whitaker, 1874– (irregular).

This work was the precursor of *British Books in Print*. Contains much publication and price information on Steinbeck works published in Britain.

Romano, Ronald F. *Collecting Old & Rare Books*. San Diego, Calif.: Kensington Press, 1979. 71p.

Intended as an introductory guide to book collecting. As such it stimulates the reader into a further appreciation of books and book collecting, and presents information useful to the aspiring collector.

Salinas Public Library. *John Steinbeck, A Guide to the Collection of the Salinas Public Library*. Edited by John Gross and Lee Richard Hayman. Salinas, Calif.: The Salinas Public Library, 1979. 196p.

An extensive listing of Steinbeck materials including first and other editions. Bibliographically descriptive information is limited.

Stanford University Libraries. *A Catalogue of the John Steinbeck Collection at Stanford University*. Compiled and edited by Susan F. Riggs. Stanford, Calif.: The Stanford University Libraries, 1980. 194p.

Of marginal value to collectors, but of great value to scholars. This catalog is useful to collectors in the sense that it identifies some Steinbeck titles that are now out of circulation. Very heavily oriented toward Steinbeck's correspondence.

The Steinbeck Collector. San Jose, Calif.: Bibliographic Research Library, 1979–.

Issued irregularly, this periodical is designed to assist Steinbeck collectors in all aspects of the collection process. Includes brief articles and various listings. Available from the Bibliographic Research Library, 964 Chapel Hill Way, San Jose, California 95122.

Steinbeck Quarterly. Muncie, Ind.: John Steinbeck Society of America, English Dept., Ball State University, 1968–.

Along with scholarly articles and book reviews, this publication provides a great deal of information of value to collectors. Available from the John Steinbeck Society of America, English Dept., Ball State University, Muncie, Indiana 47306.

Tannen, Jack. *How to Identify and Collect American First Editions: A Guide Book*. New York: Arco, 1976. 147p.

A handy guide to determining first editions and to the essential tools and minimum knowledge needed by collectors.

Tanselle, G. Thomas. "The Literature of Book Collecting," in *Book Collecting: A Modern Guide*. Edited by Jean Peters. New York: Bowker, 1977. Pp. 209–271.

This article is a must if you want to expand your knowledge of book collecting sources. Dr. Tanselle covers a great deal in a very readable way.

Texas University Humanities Research Center. *John Steinbeck: An Exhibition of American and Foreign Editions*. Austin: Humanities Research Center, University of Texas at Austin, 1963. 31p.

A basic listing of Steinbeck first editions with some descriptive bibliographic information up to 1962. An excellent source for foreign language editions other than Goldstone/Payne.

United States Library of Congress. *A Catalog of Books...* Washington, D.C.: The United States Library of Congress, 1942–.

Since 1953 known as the *National Union Catalog* because it includes materials from libraries other than the Library of Congress. Published in various sets, this work is arranged by main entries, including author, corporate bodies, etc. There is a subject catalog covering 1950 to the present. This exhaustive work is the main source for bibliographical data on various Steinbeck editions. It is available in most libraries.

Whitaker's Cumulative Book List, a Classified List of Publications. London: Whitaker, 1924–.

Each issue has two sections: a classified list of recent publications, and an alphabetical list by authors, titles, and some subjects. Full bibliographical detail, including prices, is given in both sections.

Wilson, Robert A. *Modern Book Collecting*. New York: Knopf, 1980. 270p.

Provides advice on collecting books, ranging from what to collect and where to find it, to how to tell a first edition from a reprint. Offers tips and suggestions on many facets of book collecting.

Zempel, Edward N. and Linda A. Verkler. *A First Edition?...* Peoria, Ill.: The Spoon River Press, 1977. [170p.]

Comprised of statements from 550 publishers detailing the methods they use to designate first editions. Arranged alphabetically by publisher with cross-references for publishers who have changed names or been absorbed by other companies. This work demonstrates the rampant and confusing lack of standardization in denoting first editions.

Index

Note: Main entries in the Descriptive Alphabetical List of Steinbeck Editions are set in **boldface**. Articles or short stories appearing in periodicals or in other works are set in *italics*. Brief notes needed for clarity are contained within parentheses. The lower case "n" appearing before a page number indicates that the item appears in the Notes section.

A

B

C

D

I

J

K

L

N

O

P

Q

R

T

U

V

W

Y

Z